The Company Secretary's HANDBOOK

The Company Secretary's HANDBOOK

4th edition

A Guide to Duties & Responsibilities

Helen Ashton

RECOMMENDED BY
INSTITUTE OF DIRECTORS

KOGAN
PAGE

This book has been endorsed by the Institute of Directors

The endorsement is given to selected Kogan Page books which the IoD recognises as being of specific interest to its members and providing them with up-to-date, informative and practical resources for creating business success. Kogan Page books endorsed by the IoD represent the most authoritative guidance available on a wide range of subjects including management, finance, marketing, training and HR.

The views expressed in this book are those of the author and are not necessarily the same as those of the Institute of Directors

Legal editor: Mark Stevens

First published in 1995
Second edition 2000
Third edition 2004
Fourth edition 2006

Kogan Page Limited
120 Pentonville Road
London N1 9JN
United Kingdom
www.kogan-page.co.uk

© Helen Ashton 1995, 2000, 2004, 2006

British Library Cataloguing in Publication Data

A CIP record for this book is available from the British Library.

ISBN 0 7494 4755 9

Typeset by Saxon Graphics Ltd, Derby
Printed and bound in the United States by Thomson-Shore, Inc

Contents

Introduction

This is a practical handbook to help the company secretary of a private limited company. It is designed as an introduction to the basic aspects of compliance required by the Companies Act 1985 (as amended by the Companies Act 1989). The references to the obligations of listed plcs are primarily to illustrate both models for good practice and matters that may impact on some private companies, especially if they are part of a listed group.

The main responsibilities of the company secretary are outlined together with the core duties. Record keeping and statutory compliance are subject to inspection by people outside the company and by regulatory bodies. Automatic penalties are now imposed by Companies House when company accounts are filed late. This guide is designed to help you avoid the omissions which are now subject to strict liability. For example, failure to file accounts by the due date will lead to a penalty which is automatic rather than discretionary. Where possible, checklists have been included to summarize the procedural steps necessary to effect certain changes. Companies House *Forms*, draft notices and resolutions have been included, by way of example, to help ease the administrative burden.

Directors and secretaries of private limited companies may use this guide when they do not have access to the services of a chartered secretary or in-house lawyer. Residents' associations using a limited company to hold the freehold of their property may find this a useful reference work, as will some incorporated charities. As an introduction to company secretarial practice, it may also be useful for students who are embarking on the examinations of certain professional bodies where company law or secretarial practice forms part of the syllabus.

The legislation referred to in this book is as stated at 1 September 2005. The Company Law Reform Bill was published on 3 November 2005 and had a second reading on 20 January 2006. The book includes comments on new legislation, including the European Public Limited Company Regulations 2004 (effective 8 October 2004), the draft Regulations Reform (Execution of Deeds and Documents) Order 2005 (effective 15 September 2005) and the Companies (Defective Accounts) (Authorised Person) Order 2005 (SI 2005/699), International Accounting Standards and the Companies (Audit, Investigations and Community Enterprise) Act, and comments on proposals under the Companies Bill and the Community Interest Company Regulations 2005 (SI 2005/1788) (in force 1 July 2005).

This book is not intended to replace professional advice entirely as each company will require individual attention to its problems. If problems arise, the advice of a chartered secretary or solicitor should be sought. However, this guide should help to prevent problems arising during the day-to-day administration of the company. In particular, it will assist you in getting things right from the start as even minor omissions can prove very costly.

Acknowledgement

The forms are Crown copyright. Reproduction with the permission of the Controller of Her Majesty's Stationery Office.

Please note that photocopying of the forms in this book and their subsequent submission to Companies House for registration purposes is strictly forbidden. Companies House will only accept forms for filing that meet their criteria. Please telephone Companies House (0870 3333636) and request them to send you any forms that are required. Many of the most frequently used forms are available on the Companies House website (www.companieshouse.gov.uk).

Electronic forms are being accepted by Companies House from businesses registered under its electronic filing scheme. Since this service is constantly evolving, you should consult the Companies House website for details. Only introductory information has been included about electronic filing.

1

Duties of a company secretary

Currently all public and private limited companies are required by law to appoint a company secretary (s.283(1) CA 1985). Recent events have resulted in a host of legislation and regulations that impact on the role of the company secretary, from the Cadbury Committee to the Higgs Review. The company secretary must ensure that the company has the right corporate governance procedures and processes in place, which means they must have the correct understanding of these requirements. The selection and recruitment of the appointee is the responsibility of the board of directors. The company secretary is the company's senior administrative officer and as such is charged with a wide range of duties. In addition, the company secretary is responsible for the corporate governance of the company and will need to apply the principles of best practice described in *The Combined Code*, June 2004.

The requirement to appoint a company secretary is not mandatory under the Company Law Review for private companies. However, the tasks remain for smaller private companies and still need to be carried out. Larger private companies also need someone to take responsibility for these tasks and they may choose to appoint a nominated individual.

The secretary, as an officer of the company, may be criminally liable with the directors for defaults. Failures to file notification of any change in the directors or the annual return form at Companies House can lead to civil penalties. Under the Insolvency Act 1986 a company secretary may also be required to make out a statement of the company's affairs when a winding-up order is made, or if an administrative receiver, or a provisional liquidator is appointed. Additionally, the Act gives the court sweeping powers to award damages against every officer of the company, including the secretary, for any breach of trust or duty, particularly in relation to the company's assets.

Companies House now enforces strict time limits for the filing of accounts and imposes automatic fines on the company if they are submitted late. In addition to complying with the requirements of company law, the company secretary may be responsible for ensuring that the company adheres to a host of ever-increasing legislation. There is a tendency by the European Union and UK Government to legislate in areas that affect the running of businesses. As an officer of the company, the secretary is charged with the responsibility of being up to date and knowledgeable about changes in the law that may affect the company and its administration.

The company secretary's responsibilities may include: administration of personnel matters; employment legislation compliance; accounting and finance duties; insurances and intellectual property rights (trade marks and patents). It is important to check your company's public file at Companies House to make sure there are no unauthorized changes. Companies House offers a monitoring service (PROOF), which provides by e-mail copies of documents filed by the company. Through custom, the company secretary's core responsibilities can be identified, and these are summarized in Table 1.1 below.

Table 1.1   Summary of the company secretary's duties

Duty	Description
Compliance with internal regulations and legislation	Checking that the company complies with: – Memorandum and Articles of Association and that these are up to date – the Companies Act 1985 – company and other legislation, eg UK Listing Rules and Regulatory on News Announcements.*
Maintenance of records	Keeping the company's statutory books and records, including registers of: – mortgages and charges – directors and secretary – directors' interests (copies of directors' service contracts and disclosable interests)

Duty	Description
	– members – debenture holders – in the case of a public company, keeping a register of interests in voting shares – keeping the company seal.
Administration of board and general meetings, sub committees of the board, eg Remuneration committee, Nomination committee, the Audit committee and the Executive committee	Procedural compliance and administration in: – helping the chair to set agendas, preparing papers for the board and committees – preparing and sending out notices – attendance at board meetings and taking minutes and keeping the minute books – ensuring the Combined Code and UK Listing Rules are observed* – retention of Documents and setting an Information Retention Policy.
Compliance – filing forms etc at Companies House	This must be done within the time limits given. Particular importance is attached to filing company accounts and returns, together with notices of changes to registers, eg charges, resolutions adopted by shareholder resolution at general meetings. – Generally completing Companies House Forms. – Notifying regulatory governing bodies, including, where relevant, Stock Exchange, and the Securities and Exchange Commission (SEC).
Collation of accounts and compliance with legislation	Ensuring that: – the company's accounting records are maintained in accordance with company legislation, and that there is a sound system of internal controls with at least a bi-annual review of controls* – the company's accounting records are prepared in time – signing directors' report in the company's accounts – the company's accounting records are in the form required by company law and accounting standards – copies of accounts are distributed to the appropriate persons within the correct time constraints – the accounts have the disclosures required by the Combined Code, Turnbull Requirements under

Table 1.1   continued

Duty	Description
	the US Sarbanes–Oxley Act 2002 and the Listing Rules and other relevant bodies eg the United States Securities and Exchange Commission.*
Shareholder communications	Issuing: – circulars – dividends – documentation concerning shares generally (eg share transfers) – notices of meetings.
Access to records	Ensuring that eligible persons can review company records and that the company is compliant with the Data Protection Act and Information Retention Requirements.
Legal and corporate governance regulatory advice	– Ensuring that the board considers employees and other stakeholders when decisions are made. – Advising directors on their legal responsibilities and updating them on developments in the law, corporate governance developments and corporate social responsibility concerning the running of companies. – Advising on board procedures. – Ensuring that board decisions have considered implementation issues, tax accounting and business finance consequences. – That the Memorandum and Articles of Association are complied with and kept up to date.
Share administration	Managing and supervising: – the register of members – share transfer matters generally – requests for information from shareholders – the issue of share and debenture certificates – the notice of allotments and restructuring to Companies House – employee share schemes/options.
Information link	Maintaining communication links between: – the chair, directors and non-executive directors – shareholders and the board – employees and the board – media/press and the company.

Duty	Description
Running the registered office	Administering the registered office: — dealing with correspondence — receipt and care of official documents — making documents required by law available for inspection by third parties — ensuring the company's name is displayed at the registered offices.
Security of documentation	Managing the security of: — company seal — Certificate of Incorporation — Certificate(s) on Change of Name — Memorandum and Articles of Association — directors' service contracts — share certificates and stock transfer forms — other documents of title.
Health and safety	Where a business has more than five employees it must: — Produce a written health and safety policy (and keep it up to date). — Have a process for putting the policy into practice. — Explain the policy to the employees and develop a prevention. — Ensure there is a regular assessment of work-related risks by a competent person. — Provide employees with relevant and sufficient information about health and safety risks, and training on preventative measures. — Appoint health and safety representatives. — Have measures to deal with serious and imminent danger to people in the company. — See www.hse.gov.uk for further details.

* Applies to publicly listed companies and relevant subsidiaries (which may be private limited companies)

If the company secretary is an employee of the company, his or her contract of employment may specify additional duties apart from those in Table 1.1. In general, any extra responsibilities will depend on the type of company in which the secretary works and any regulations governing that particular industry. If employed by a small to medium-sized company, you may be expected to be familiar with additional legal obligations.

As an officer, the company secretary has ostensible authority to bind the company in contracts relating to the company's administration, in the same way that a director can. The scope of his or her express authority may, however, vary from company to company. He or she can also certify copy documents (in particular, minutes and written resolutions) and is authorized under the Companies Act to sign *Forms* and notices. The company secretary may also sign the report of directors and witness the use of the seal, when authorized by the board. Where the use of the company seal has been deregulated, the signatures of a director and the secretary of the company can be used for the purposes of executing a document with the same effect as using the seal. Companies House publishes a leaflet called *Directors' and Secretaries' Guide GBA1* available free of charge either by post or via its website (www.companieshouse.gov.uk).

The company secretary in their capacity as adviser to the board has additional responsibility classified by the Companies (Audit, Investigations and Committee Enterprise) Act 2004. An auditor will expect the company secretary (or other persons with information about the company) to disclose relevant information for an audit. The secretary needs to ensure professional advice is taken by the board if he or she suspects wrongful trading. They will also need to ensure that the board disclose information such as threatened litigation, withdrawal of credit by a bank, or other relevant audit information.

Assistant and deputy secretaries

In the Companies Act 1985 the role of an assistant secretary or deputy secretary is mentioned. If not prohibited by the Companies Articles of Association, a deputy or assistant secretary can be appointed in the same way as a company secretary.

It is not clearly stated whether it is a requirement to notify Companies House of the appointment of a deputy or an assistant secretary as they generally just record secretaryships.

Joint secretaries

The Companies Act states that the requirement to advise Companies House of an appointment or resignation of a secretary also applies to joint secretaries. The details of joint secretaries must also be recorded in the Register of Secretaries. Joint secretaries will have joint authority and must sign with the other company secretary unless expressly stated in the Articles of Association.

Signing on behalf of the company

The company secretary is usually authorized by the board to sign for administrative matters on behalf of them. By statute the secretary can sign certain returns to Companies House and usually signs the report of the directors on behalf of the board, although this can also be signed by a director. The new draft Regulatory Return (Execution of Deeds and Documents) Order 2005 is designed to simplify and clarify the signing of deeds and documents by corporations. The current Law of Property Act 1925 requires the signature of a director and a secretary, and The Companies Act 1985 permits a deed to be signed by two officers. These Acts both restrict the officers as natural persons, thus limiting those corporations that are also officers. The order removes the company secretary requirement and affirms the validity of two directors. As of September 2005, companies that are officers are able to be represented by authorized persons.

2

Types of company

This chapter gives a basic outline of what types of company exist and what other legal trading structures can be used for business purposes. Before embarking on acquiring a company, you should seek professional advice, in particular tax advice to ensure that the type of company you wish to form is the most tax effective.

Historically, various types of company have developed and the following are referred to in the companies legislation:

1. Public limited company;
2. Private limited company;
3. Company limited by guarantee;
4. Private unlimited company;
5. Overseas companies – registered either as:
   (i) a branch;
   (ii) a place of business; or
   (iii) a financial institution (which includes entities other than companies);
6. Limited Liability Partnerships (LLP);
7. Societas Europaea (SE);
8. Community Interest Companies (CICs).

In addition, there are other types of incorporated body which exist such as friendly societies and industrial and provident societies.

These organizations have a separate registry which is administered by the Registrar of Friendly Societies. Different rules govern their administration.

When registering a CIC the documents must be as specified by the CIC regulator. This information can be found at www.cicregulator.gov.uk. A CIC company must pass a 'community interest test' if it wishes to register as a CIC and it will need to demonstrate annually how its work has helped the community. The CIC regulator will ensure that these companies comply with their statutory requirements.

Various types of business structure may be used by entrepreneurs who may choose to carry on in business either as a sole trader, in partnerships or through private and public companies. There is currently a legal requirement that every company must have a company secretary as well as the statutory minimum number of directors. At least two people must be involved in the running of a company, one of whom must be the company secretary and the other a director. Companies have a separate legal personality from their owners and may in their own right, for example, own property and hold a bank account. A company is operated by directors for the benefit of its shareholders. The shareholders' rights are regulated by companies legislation, by the Memorandum and Articles of Association, and by any agreement that the shareholders may make between themselves. Shares represent funds invested in the business and share certificates are issued as evidence of ownership of shares.

As stated previously, this book is designed to help company secretaries of private companies to deal in particular with the requirements of the Companies Act 1985. Private limited companies have many statutory responsibilities including the maintenance of statutory books, accounting records, the filing of annual returns and accounts.

The Companies Act 1985 provides for two main categories of company: public companies and private companies. A private company can be limited by shares, limited by guarantee or unlimited.

Public limited companies

The Companies Act 1985, s1(3) defines a public company as one limited by shares or limited by guarantee and having a share capital, whose Memorandum states that it is to be a public company and which was registered or re-registered as a public company under the provisions of the 1985 Act or former Companies Acts. However, since 22 December 1980, no public company may be formed as, or become, a guarantee company.

The main differences between a public and a private company arise from the requirements with which a public company must comply in order to register. The main differences are that: the company's name must end with the words public limited company or plc (or in the Welsh equivalent Cwmni Cyfyngedig Cyhoedduss or CCC); the company's Memorandum must be in the form specified for such a company (Table F) and the nominal value of its allotted share capital must not be less than the authorized minimum of £50,000 (a minimum 25 per cent [plus any premium] paid up on issue). When a public limited company is also a community interest company the name will end: 'community interest public limited company' or 'community interest plc' (or, in the Welsh equivalent 'cwmni buddiant cymunedol cyhoeddus cyfyngedig' or 'cwmni buddiant cymunedol ccc'). A public company must also have at least two members and two directors. Their shares or debentures may be offered to the general public (through the Stock Exchange if the company's shares are listed on the London Stock Exchange). A newly incorporated public limited company may not commence trading until it has received a certificate to do so from the Registrar (s.117 CA 1985).

The advantage of a public over a private company is that the former has the right to offer shares or debentures to the public (for cash or otherwise). In return for this benefit, public companies are subject to far more stringent controls than private companies.

The company secretary of a public company must be suitably qualified in accordance with the requirements of s286 of the Companies Act 1985 which details the suitable professional qualifications. Directors of public companies must ensure that the company secretary or joint secretary is a person who has the requisite knowledge and experience to carry out the role. A company secretary must meet the following requirements:

1. On 22 December 1980 have held the office of secretary (or assistant or deputy secretary) of the company; or

2. For three of the five years immediately prior to this appointment have held the office of secretary of a company other than a private company; or

3. Be a member of one of the following professional bodies:

   a) the Institute of Chartered Secretaries and Administrators
   b) the Institute of Chartered Accountants (England and Wales, Scotland or Ireland)
   c) the Chartered Association of Certified Accountants
   d) the Institute of Cost and Management Accountants
   e) the Chartered Institute of Public Finance and Accountancy; or

4. Be a barrister, advocate or solicitor called or admitted in any part of the United Kingdom; or

5. Be a person who, by virtue of holding or having held any other position or being a member of any other body appears to the directors to be capable of discharging these functions.

Because public companies are beyond the scope of this publication, the additional responsibilities of the company secretary of a public company are only outlined to a limited degree and not discussed in any detail.

Where a public limited company has been formed abroad, the company will need to apply for branch registration if it establishes one brand in the UK. An overseas public company will be subject to the rules of Financial Services and Markets Act 2000 and the city Code on Takeovers and Mergers.

Private limited companies

A private company is any company that is not public, ie they cannot offer their shares or debentures to the public. Profits are distributed to shareholders by way of a dividend as with public companies. They are also subject to the regulations of the Companies Acts in return for the benefits of limited liability. Private limited companies are the type of company most frequently incorporated.

Companies limited by guarantee

Guarantee companies do not have a share capital. They are usually formed by operators of clubs and associations for charitable, social or other non-profit-making purposes. The structure of the company at board level is the same as for a private limited company (ie it must have at least one director and the company secretary). The Articles of Association may sometimes refer to the directors as executive officers or to a council of management, but the duties and responsibilities of the officers are the same as those of directors.

Guarantee companies have members not shareholders. However, historically guarantee companies could have a share capital, but this is not possible nowadays. Guarantee company members are different from shareholders in that each member undertakes to contribute to the assets of the company in the event that it is wound up while he or she is a member. In practice, the sum guaranteed by the member is often £1. On liquidation each member would have to pay this guarantee of £1. The member is not obliged to pay the sum guaranteed while the company is a going concern; the liability only arises if a contribution is needed to pay the company's debts while it is being liquidated. Guarantee companies normally have a non-profit distribution clause in the Articles of Association which will prohibit the payment of dividends and for the distribution of assets on a winding up.

Societas Europaea (SE)

The European Company Statute and European Limited-liability Regulations 2004 (effective 8 October 2004) together with a directive concerning worker involvement called Societas Europaea (SE) came into force at the same time. In the UK, Companies House can register an SE. An SE is created by a holding company or the merger of companies in a minimum of two EU States. It can also be created by the conversion of a company registered in the UK. The directive on employee involvement requires that there are negotiations with employees and a body is established to represent the employees' views.

The European Society Europaea does have the benefit in that it might be a useful mechanism for cross-border mergers with companies from other EU States. There is a new guidance booklet published by Companies House about forming a Societas Europaea – GB06 and this can be obtained from their website at www.companieshouse.gov.uk. The registration fee for an SE either by a merger or as a subsidiary is £20.

Other types of company

Another type of company which can be registered under the Companies Act is the unlimited company. As the name implies, there is no limit to the liability of the shareholders. Consequently, unlimited liability companies are not widely used. These companies do not have to file annual accounts (although there are exceptions to this). A key advantage is that, subject to their articles, such companies can reduce their issued share capital in any way. The reduction of share capital, or purchase of own shares, is far more tightly regulated for limited liability companies and subject to complex rules. Both guarantee companies and unlimited companies are sometimes formed for sporting events, to enable the organizers to take advantage of the separate, distinct, legal personality.

A business does not always need to be incorporated. An entrepreneur may choose to be a sole trader or to operate in partnership. A sole trader, as the name implies, is a business effectively run by one person – the owner. The life of this business extends to the life of the owner and does not have a separate identity. There is no limit to the liability of the individual.

Partnerships occur where two or more people carry on a business together. A partnership may be created by a formal written partnership agreement or by an informal verbal agreement. An analysis of the differences between partnerships, private limited companies and limited liability partnerships is summarized in Table 2.1 below.

Table 2.1 Summary of differences between companies and partnerships

Registered private limited company

Incorporated	Unincorporated Partnerships	Limited Liability (LLP)
The company has a separate legal identity – the company can, for example, sue in its own name	There is no separate legal identity – partners are jointly and severally less liable for the debts of the partnership – special procedural rules allow the business to sue, or be sued, in the name of the partnership	There is a separate legal identity – not severally and joint liability for partnership – own regulation of a membership agreement (optional) – Articles of Association
Has to comply with incorporation formalities (eg the Companies Act deed 1985) – expense, incorporation costs	Formed informally, by word – may or may not attract formation expenses	– expense, incorporation costs
Company accounts are open to the public at Companies House – must file annual returns	Partnership accounts are private	File accounts and open to the public at Companies House
Internal flexibility – can change objects by special resolution passed with the agreement of those shareholders who hold 75 per cent of the voting rights	The constitution of the partnership can be changed by agreement	Membership agreement needs complete approval*
Profits subject to Corporation Tax (payable by company)	Profits subject to Income Tax (payable by partners)	Profits subject to Income Tax for individual partners (but where the partners are corporations, profits are subject to Corporation Tax)
Shareholders do not, in their own right, have any executive function	Partners usually take an active part in the business	Designated partners are executives and non-designated partners have no effective function
Perpetual succession	Partnership ends on death/removal, etc of a partner (depends on agreement)	Succession

*but changes to the articles are similar to a company

Note that it is not within the scope of this book to cover in detail limited partnerships and limited liability partnerships.

The limits of liability

In the case of a private limited company, the liability of a member is usually limited to the amount contributed for his or her shares, or any amount owing on those shares. As discussed above, companies limited by guarantee have their liability limited to the amount members have agreed to guarantee in the event of the company being wound up.

There are a number of statutory exceptions to the doctrine of members' limited liability and in leading cases attention has been drawn to the economic reality behind the legal framework. When the protection of limited liability is lifted by the court, the shareholders may be deemed jointly and severally liable for the debts of the company. The modern practice is increasingly for financial obligations to be laid at the door of the company's officers. For example, a bank lending to a company will often require personal guarantees from the directors or the shareholders. This negates the advantage of limited liability to a large extent.

Directors and other officers may not be able to limit their personal liability by sheltering behind the company (for example, recent environmental legislation attributes personal liability to directors as well as to the company itself). Increasing pressures from the European Union for environmental protection, adverse publicity and public pressure arising from cases such as BCCI, Polly Peck and more recently Enron and Worldcom mean that officers of a company are likely to face an ever-increasing barrage of legislation. Gross negligence which results in death may give rise to a charge of corporate manslaughter. The consultation document *Corporate Manslaughter – the Government's draft Bill for reform* was published in March 2005. This will create a new criminal offence for corporate manslaughter. Senior management will be directly responsible for the deaths of people caused by poor health and safety. Evidence in the new Corporate Manslaughter Bill was heard by the House of Commons Select Committee on 24 October 2005. The law is now being changed following a series of high-profile rail accidents where the current offence of corporate manslaughter was considered insufficient.

Like any other officer of the company, the secretary owes fiduciary duties to the company similar to those owed by a director. No provision in the company's Articles or otherwise which purports to exempt the secretary (or any other officer) from liability in respect of negligence, default, breaches of duty or trust can be enforced. As with other officers, the secretary should always take care not to place him, or herself in the position where personal liability for his or her actions cannot be denied.

The secretary should be aware that liability can be incurred even in circumstances where he or she has not personally been responsible, for example, a default in compliance in statutory filing requirements.

3

Formation of companies

There are two ways of setting up a private limited company. You can either form a company from scratch or buy a ready made company 'off the shelf'. Whichever method you choose, you will first have to decide what the proposed company's name will be, who will be the officers and shareholders, and what the company will do.

Checking company names

Once you have chosen the name of your company, you need to find out if the name is available for use. Since over 4 million companies have been registered at Companies House, it is possible that the name you propose to use (or a similar name) is already on the Register of Companies.

Whether you decide to form one from scratch or buy a company off the shelf, it is essential that the name used is sufficiently different from any existing name. This is because companies already registered can object to the Registrar if they feel that the new name is similar enough to cause confusion. The Registrar can then direct your company to change its name, something nobody wants in the first few months of trading. Where a company name is too similar to one already registered you can be required to change your company name within 12 months of registration. In certain circumstances this can be extended to five years.

It is also important that the name you choose conforms to the statutory requirements. A company name must, for example, end in the correct suffix of its type – 'Public Limited Company' or an abbreviation (or the Welsh equivalent), 'Limited' or 'Ltd' (in a private limited company), or 'Commonhold Association Limited' for a commonhold association (or the Welsh equivalent). Companies that are community interest companies must end as 'Community Interest Public Company' or as 'Community Interest Company' or use the abbreviations 'CIC' (or the Welsh equivalent). The use of certain words is also governed by separate legislation, eg Nurses and Nursing. In these situations you will need to ensure that you comply with the statutory requirements.

It is also worth noting that a mighty company can crush weak ones. Public companies and larger groups of limited companies monitor the index of companies to ensure that use of their own name is not being infringed. Lawyers, trade mark agents and records agents are increasingly instructed to monitor a company name. Such companies will not hesitate to start a 'passing off' action against those who dare to use too similar a name. To fight such an action can be expensive, time-wasting and could prove fatal to a new business. Passing off proceedings are not, of course, limited to large companies and any company with an interest to protect may take this action. Now that the estimated number of enterprises in the UK is over four million (DTI Annual Report, 2003–4), this is increasingly important.

How to check a name

The first thing to remember is that certain words do not count when judging similarity of names. These include: 'the', 'and', 'company', 'limited', 'public limited company', and any abbreviation (eg Co, Ltd, plc, &, etc). So **The Universal Widget Company Limited** would be considered by the Registrar to be the same as **Universal Widget Limited** and would not be accepted for registration.

As company secretary you will also need to consider similar sounding names. It is worth drawing up a list of phonemes to check against the Register as seen in Table 3.1.

Table 3.1   Carrying out a company name check

Selected name	Similar names
Gin and Tonic Limited	Gym and Tonic
	Gene and Tunic
	Gyn and Tannic
	Glyn and Thionic
	Gin, Tonic and Lemon
	G&T
	Jim & Tonik
	Djinn and Ptonic (!)
	etc (there can be many)

Any company registration agent will usually check your chosen name for you if you buy off the shelf. However, you need to ask them what checks they will make. Some agents limit their liability by stating that they will check only for identical names, for example. If you want a trade mark search (see below), this will usually have to be requested specifically. If in doubt, you should also use the Patents Office Advisory service or a trade mark agent, who will give you an opinion as to the advisability of using a particular name. Alternatively, you can check the name yourself by carrying out a search on the index of names at Companies House in London, Cardiff, Edinburgh or one of its satellite offices, or by using Companies House on the internet (www.companieshouse.gov.uk) or a search agent's website.

There are also certain words and expressions, the registration of which is prohibited under the Companies Act 1985 unless approval for use is obtained from the Secretary of State before registration. A company name must not be misleading or offensive. Regulations govern the use of certain words in a name, for example 'international', 'holdings', and 'group'. Some words are restricted in use by other legislation, for example 'architect', 'dentist', 'optician', 'insurance broker', 'Sheffield'. A list of all these types of restricted words and phrases is set out in a Companies House leaflet, *Company Names – GBF2*.

Bear in mind that certain words may be protected by being registered as trade marks. A trade mark search can be carried out, either by an agent, or in person, at the Patent Office in London. It can be cheaper to do this in person as the staff in this office are very helpful and the computerized database will easily aid you in investigating your name.

Trade mark searches can also be carried out on the websites of search agents.

You will also need to check to see if the chosen name is being used as a domain name on the internet.

As company secretary it is worth checking that the name of your company is sufficiently dissimilar to other registrations as it is noticeable that companies are becoming more litigious in protecting their names. You also may not wish to be associated with companies of dubious reputation which may be insolvent, or worse.

Further, the Registrar can refuse to register a company name if the name is the same or considered to be the same as an existing company name. The Registrar can ignore the use of the word 'and' or an '&'. After registration a company that is already registered can object to your new company's name if it is considered to be 'too like' their company name.

There is also the risk that a business is using your name prior to your registration as a trading name but has not registered a trade mark. In this scenario, the business using the trading name may choose to bring an action for 'passing off'.

A separate check should also be made at the Trade Mark Registry to ensure that the new name does not conflict with a registered mark. The Trade Mark Registry can be viewed online at www.patent.gov.uk. Checking trade marks needs advice and this can be obtained from the Patent Office Trade Mark Service or from a Registered Trade Mark Agent.

Domain names

Registering an internet domain site is separate from Companies House and the Trade Mark Registry. If you need a domain address you must register this as soon as possible to avoid disappointment!

Incorporation

In certain circumstances it is easier to buy a company off the shelf than to incorporate one from scratch. However, just like buying a suit, not everyone wants one off the peg, but one individually tailored to meet their needs.

The main differences are time and cost. It may take less time and prove less expensive to get a ready-made company up and running. The advantage of a 'special incorporation' is that you can start the life of the company with your chosen name and with a constitution tailored to your needs. You can also choose the original share subscribers and officers. Companies House offers a 'same day' incorporation service at the premium rate of £50 for those companies that need to be incorporated quickly. Electronic incorporations are now available for £15 and paper incorporations are £20. Limited Liability Partnerships (LLPs) are the same level as for companies. Companies House has introduced a new LLP 'same day' registration service for £50.

In order to incorporate a company from scratch, you will need the following documents signed and completed:

1. *Form 10*
2. *Form 12* (sworn before a Commissioner of Oaths, Notary public, JP or a solicitor)
3. Memorandum and Articles of Association
4. Incorporation fee

These items will need to be filed at Companies House.

Business consideration

Before you incorporate a company, you must consider what is the most important structure for the business. The new company or appropriate business structure needs to be tailored to your needs. Sometimes agreements and undertakings are required before a company is registered. A shareholders' agreement may also be appropriate to protect a minority shareholder, for dispute resolution or simply to set down internal management arrangements. Similarly, where there are two shareholders who hold 50 per cent each, an agreement may be appropriate to cater for scenarios where there is deadlock. Indeed, one can form companies with 'deadlock' articles. Shareholders' agreements are private and can be used to ensure that confidential internal arrangements do not appear on the public record.

Evidence of incorporation of a company is the Certificate of Incorporation issued by the Registrar when the appropriate documents are presented and approved. This certificate is, in effect, the company's birth certificate. The date given on the certificate is the date on which the company is formed and from which it can properly trade. The name shown on the certificate is the name by which the company must be known and can only be changed by a special resolution. With effect from 1 September 1999, all new companies have to have their names shown in upper case only on the Certificate of Incorporation or on Change of Name. The number on the certificate is specific to the company and will never change throughout its life.

There is only one original Certificate of Incorporation of a company, issued by Companies House. If it is lost, a duplicate may be obtained from the Registrar on payment of a fee. Electronic certificates are supplied for companies using the e-incorporation service. It is important that the original certificate is kept in a safe place. A company may be called upon many times to produce the original certificate, especially when a bank account is being opened.

Buying a company off the shelf

All you need to do is to contact a company registration agent who will either sell you a ready-made 'off-the-shelf' company, or carry out a special formation for you. For ready-made companies, the registration agent can arrange for the company's Memorandum and Articles of Association (its constitution), to be amended as necessary. Special formations require names and business activities to be given to the agent at the outset. Alternatively, your accountants or lawyers may have a specialist company secretarial department which can deal with this on your behalf.

The agent will require: details of the registered office address and completed company *Form 288a* (see page 129), giving details of the new officers (at least one director and a secretary). If you are happy to use the name of a company already incorporated by the agent, and no amendments to the constitution are required, on payment of the agent's fee the company will be transferred. You will also need to have at least one proposed shareholder for a private company. You will be supplied with the items in Table 3.2 for an off-the-shelf company.

Note that plcs have slightly different requirements. In particular, they need a certificate to trade from the Registrar confirming that their minimum paid-up share capital is one quarter of £50,000.

You should be aware that there are additional forms that need to be filed, for example *Form 225* to change the accounts reference date (see Chapter 4).

The company registration agent will normally file any notifications to the Registrar required to hand the company over to you. You should, however, check that all the relevant documents have been filed at Companies House, in particular the notification of change in registered office address.

Businesses that file a large number of forms may register with Companies House and participate in its electronic filing scheme. There are now a number of forms that can be filed electronically (see the Companies House website for details).

Memorandum and Articles of Association

The constitution and internal regulations of a company are set out in its Memorandum and Articles of Association. The **Memorandum** establishes the basis of the company's existence in accordance with the Companies Act 1985. The **Articles**, on the other hand, are essentially concerned with the company's internal management and administrative structure. A company's Articles cannot modify, or have priority over, the Memorandum. Each director and shareholder should be given a copy of the Memorandum and Articles of Association. Table A was amended on 22 December 2000 by the Companies Act 1985 (Electronic Communication) Order 2006 to permit electronic communications for corporate reasons.

Table 3.2 Off-the-shelf company documentation supplied by registration agent

Off-the-shelf company documentation

1. Certificate of Incorporation
2. At least one copy of the Memorandum and Articles of Association
3. Two stock transfer forms for the subscriber shares (one only, where sole shareholder)
4. A letter of resignation of the first director and secretary of the company
5. Minutes of the first board meeting appointing the new directors and secretary, and approving the change in registered office address
6. A letter of guarantee that the company has not previously traded, signed on behalf of the registration agents
7. Copies of the forms appointing the new director(s) and secretary of the company as filed at Companies House (*Form 288a* – see page 129)
8. A copy of the form changing the registered office address as filed at Companies House (*Form 287*– see page 128)
9. A combined company register, including share certificates
10. (optional) A company seal, *Forms 88(2), 88(3)* and *225* (see pages 121, 123, and 127)

Table B of the Companies (Tables A to F) Regulations 1985, as amended gives the statutory form of a company's Memorandum of Association, setting out the company's name, main objects and situation of the registered office. Most companies will have a lengthy objects clause to cover activities that may not be deemed to be incidental to the carrying on of any trade or business, for example, applying for an Act of Parliament. Table 3.3 is a summary of the required legal contents of the Memorandum of Association.

It is quite common for the objects of a company purchased from a registration agent to be those of a general commercial company. This type of company can carry on any trade or business whatsoever, and will have the power to do all things necessary or incidental to the carrying on of any trade or business. You may wish to specify a particular core business in the objects clause of the Memorandum of Association. You can request that the agent inserts these details and limits the range of activity allowed. In some instances it may be desirable or necessary to specify precisely the objects for which the company is formed.

Table 3.3 A summary of the contents of the Memorandum of Association

Clause number	Particulars
1.	The full name of the company. 'Limited' must be the last word in the case of a company limited by shares or guarantee (with exceptions)
2.	The situation of the registered office (England and Wales, or Scotland)
3.	The company's objects
4.	A statement that the liability of the members is limited
5.	The authorised share capital
Last page	The name(s) and address(es) of the first shareholder(s) or subscriber(s)

A company can change its objects, subject to the provisions in the Companies Act 1985, by passing a special resolution (75 per cent majority of those who vote) at a general meeting of the shareholders (see Chapter 8).

Acknowledging the importance of the Articles of Association, the legislature has offered guidance by the provision of model regulations for limited companies. The Articles typically include provisions governing the allotment and transfer of shares, the proceedings for general meetings, quorum requirements, the exercise of voting rights and for the appointment and removal of directors.

Table A of the Companies (Tables A to F) Regulations 1985 is a statutory model for a private company's Articles of Association. The company may adopt all or any of the regulations contained in Table A. If a company does not register its own Articles of Association then Table A applies. It is normal practice, however, for a registration agent to prepare Articles of Association amending Table A. You will therefore need to obtain a copy of the relevant Table A to understand fully the amendments made to it by your Articles of Association.

The original Memorandum and Articles of Association are signed by the first shareholder(s) (subscriber(s)) on the last page of each document. The signed document is filed at Companies House with the other papers required for incorporation. Details of what to do next are given in the following chapters.

Trade mark registration of a name

It is advisable to register your new company name as a trade mark, especially when it is unusual and distinctive. A trade mark will then give you exclusive rights of the mark in appropriate classes. The mark must be distinctive for the goods and services it covers and not be similar or the same as marks already registered. The Patent Office provides an advisory service which is economical and offers advice at the onset before an application is submitted.

4

Getting started

Once you have incorporated your company, or purchased it off the shelf, you will need to organize various statutory matters. In particular, you must ensure that the company registers are written up, shares are properly issued and the necessary administration is completed.

The registered office

A company registered in England or Wales must have its registered office address in England or Wales whereas a company registered in Scotland will have its registered office in Scotland. All official and legal correspondence will be sent to this address. The registered office address is recorded at Companies House and notice of any change must be given to the relevant Registrar on *Form 287* (see page 128).

On incorporation, the first registered office address is recorded on *Form 10* (see page 116). If you have incorporated your own company you will have selected the registered office of your choice. If you have purchased your company from formation agents you will need to change the registered office address by filing *Form 287* although it is probable that the agent will undertake to do this in conjunction with the transfer of the company to you.

Changes

A change of registered office takes effect from its date of registration by the Registrar but there is a buffer zone of 14 days beginning with the date it is registered during which both the old and new addresses are valid. *Form 287* must be filed within 14 days of a board resolution resolving to change the registered office address. The company's registered office address must be disclosed on its headed notepaper (see page 30). In addition, a nameplate will need to be displayed and fixed outside every office or place that business is carried out.

Disclosure – company notepaper

It is also important that the company state its name on all business letters, all of its notices and official publications, all bills of exchange and promissory notes, endorsements, cheques and orders for money or goods purporting to be signed on or behalf of the company; all its bills, parcels, invoices and letters of credit. In addition, the company must disclose the address of its registered office and the place the company was registered, together with its company number.

Companies that are investment companies must disclose the fact and companies that are exempt from using the word 'Limited' in their name must confirm their exemption.

These regulations also apply to external communications by e-mail.

A company does not need to disclose the names of its directors on its notepaper. If it chooses to do so, however, it must give the names of **all** directors. If the company's trading address is different from its registered office, this fact must be clearly shown. Where a company is using a trading name which is not the name under which the company is registered, it will also need to disclose both names. There are special requirements for additional disclosures for certain types of companies, for example, investment companies and charities. Companies House provides leaflets entitled *Company Names – GBF2* with further information. A sample of headed notepaper for Dashwood & Sons Limited is shown in Figure 4.1.

Dashwood & Sons Limited

Felix House
Dogget Road
Chatham
Kent

Company No 145567   Registered in England and Wales
Registered Office: Felix House, Dogget Road, Chatham, Kent

Figure 4.1   Headed notepaper sample

Location

The registered office address need not be the company's headquarters or main place of business. It can be the home of an officer, or alternatively, with their consent, the address of the company's accountants or solicitors. There may be a small charge for this service. A company is obliged to keep certain of its statutory documents at its registered office address. Table 4.1 provides a checklist of the documents and their location.

Table 4.1 Checklist of documents and their locations

Documentation to be available	Location	✓
1. Register of members (index required when over 50 members)	1. Registered office 2. Other location, must be in the country of registration (eg England and Wales or Scotland) and with items 7 and 8. If at a different location, notice must be given to Companies House on *Form 353* or *Form 353a* (if held electronically)	
2. Register of charges	Registered office	
3. Copies of documents creating legal charges	Registered office	
4. Register of debenture holders	1. Registered office 2. Other location, must be in the country of registration (eg England and Wales or Scotland). If this is kept at a location other than the registered office, a *Form 190* must be filed, or a *190a* for electronic data	
5. Register of directors and secretaries	Registered office	
6. Copies of directors' service contracts or memoranda of terms	1. Registered office 2. Other location, must be in the country of registration (eg England and Wales or Scotland). If they are kept at locations other than the registered office, then a *Form 318* must be filed	
7. Register of directors' interests	1. Registered office 2. Other location, must be in the country of registration and with items 1 and 8. If kept at a location other than the registered office, a *Form 325* or *325a* (if held electronically) must be filed	

Documentation to be available	Location	✓
8. Register of substantial interests (reports under ss212, 214 and 215 CA 1985) for plcs	1. Registered office 2. Other location, must be in the country of registration and with items 1 and 7	
9. Accounting records (last three years for private companies, and six years for plcs)	1. Registered office 2. Other location, must be in Great Britain	
10. Minute book (general meeting minutes)	Registered office	
11. Copy of contract relating to the company purchasing its own shares (or memorandum of its terms) for 10 years after the transaction date	Registered office	

Note. It is useful to keep a copy of the Memorandum and Articles of Association, and amendments, at the registered office, although this is not a statutory requirement.

If the company chooses to locate the allowed items elsewhere it must notify the Registrar on the *Forms* given in Table 4.2.

Table 4.2 Summary of action required for information not held at registered office address

Statutory books/Document(s)	Action if located at other than registered office address
The register of members	*Form 353 or 353a, Register of members* (see page 136 or 137)
Copies of directors' service contracts or memoranda of contracts	*Form 318, Location of directors' service contracts* (see page 133)
Register of directors' interests	*Form 325 or 325a, Location of register of directors' interests in shares etc* (see page 134 or 135)
Register of debenture holders	*Form 190, Location of register of debenture holders* (see page 125)

The location of the registered office will affect the tax office which will deal with the company and they should be notified accordingly. Any change in the registered office may result in a change in a company's tax office and the company will also need to amend its headed notepaper. A checklist for the steps necessary to change the registered office is set out in Table 4.3.

Table 4.3 Checklist of actions on change of registered office address

Action	✓
1. Hold a board meeting to approve a resolution to change the registered office address	
2. File *Form 287* at Companies House within 14 days of (1)	
3. Amend the company's documentation that displays details of the registered address (eg headed notepaper, invoices, etc)	
4. Place a nameplate at the new address. Check that the old nameplate is removed.	
5. Advise others of the change (eg accountants, solicitors, banks, Inland Revenue, etc)	
6. Check that those statutory books that have to be held at the registered office are moved to the new address, and for others (if not located at registered office) eg register of members, check the necessary notice is given on the appropriate form (*Forms 353, 353a, 318, 325, 325a* and *190*)	

The Companies Act 1985 states that every company shall put its registered office address in its correspondence (headed notepaper, etc). In addition, when a company discloses its place of registration it can, if registered in England and Wales, use one of the following: Registered in Cardiff; Registered in England and Wales; Registered in England; Registered in London; or, Registered in Wales. A company that has been registered in Scotland may use either Registered in Scotland or Registered in Edinburgh.

Directors and secretaries

A private limited company must have at least one director who cannot also be the company secretary, ie there is a minimum requirement of two officers. The Articles of Association can prescribe a greater number to be the minimum, or maximum, number of directors allowed and must therefore be checked to ensure that any extra obligation is met.

The directors' main role is to manage and run the business for the shareholders. The directors may exercise all the powers of the company in this respect. Decisions about the day-to-day management of the company are made by the board of directors. Resolutions of the board are passed following a vote at board meetings and are recorded in the minutes. One of the company secretary's core responsibilities involves taking the board minutes and ensuring that they are properly recorded. The company secretary will also often prepare a draft agenda which is circulated to the board before the meeting, and the final version is usually approved by the chair. Financial and legal responsibility for the management and running of the company is shared by the directors. In practice, directors' powers will extend to major policy decisions on behalf of the company and they will only seek shareholder approval when required by statute or by the Memorandum and Articles of Association.

The board can delegate authority to individual directors or to a committee of directors to carry out any agreed decisions.

Appointment of directors

The first directors of the company are appointed on *Company Form 10* (see page 116) which is signed by the appointees and the subscribers to the Memorandum and Articles of Association or by the company's agents. This form is filed at Companies House together with the other initial incorporation documents.

Once the first director or directors have been appointed, the rules governing any changes to the board are set out in the company's Articles of Association. It is normal for the Articles to permit the board to approve appointment and resignation of directors. You should be aware that some Articles of Association include the provision in Table A that requires directors to retire by rotation each year at the annual general meeting. This will be discussed further in Chapter 7.

If a company has been bought off the shelf, the company formation agents will require new directors to be appointed in place of their nominees. This is done on a *Form 288a* (see page 129). The company formation agent(s) will request buyers of shelf companies to complete forms to appoint the secretary and director(s) (*Form 288a*) together with the form for change of registered office (*Form 287* – see page 128). The registration agents will give notice of the resignation of their nominee director(s) and secretary on *Forms 288b* to Companies House. Upon receipt of *Forms 288a* and *287*, the agents will provide you with a written letter of resignation of the first director and secretary, together with a board minute or written resolution appointing the new director(s) and secretary and approving the transfer of the subscribers' shares and the change of registered address. You should also receive a certificate of non-trading for the company (covering the period from incorporation to the transfer date). Note that many private companies are incorporated with a sole member.

An example of some of the documentation required in the transfer of a ready made company is shown in this chapter. Our company, Dashwood & Sons Limited, has appointed one director, Rupert Max Dashwood, and Fiona Dashwood as secretary and director, in place of the nominees. After telephoning the company registration agents, they have been provided with *Forms 288a, 288b* and *287* along with the appropriate board minutes and letters of resignation. Completed forms and minutes are shown on the following pages. Usually the documents shown in Figures 4.2 and 4.3 will be prepared by the agents.

New directors should have an induction on joining the board. Recent corporate governance reports have highlighted the need for training, especially for non-executive directors. The Higgs Report gives a good practical checklist of matters to be covered by an induction of a director, eg details of products and services, group structures, major issues and management strategy to mitigate risk, corporate contribution and board procedures, KPIs (Key Performance Indicators) and regulatory constraints, introduction to senior management, understanding major customers and suppliers and major shareholders.

Directors' residential address

If the disclosure of a director's (or a secretary's) home address creates or may cause a serious risk of violence or intimidation to that person or other people at that address, you can apply for permission not to disclose the address. New legislation was introduced after attacks on the directors of Huntingdon Life Sciences and other incidents. Under

MINUTES OF A MEETING OF DIRECTORS OF DASHWOOD & SONS LIMITED HELD AT THE OFFICES OF SPECIALIST COMPANY FORMATION AGENTS LIMITED, CITY ROAD, LONDON EC1 ON THE 6TH DAY OF APRIL 2003 at 11.00 AM

PRESENT: H Jones (representing Specialist Co Nominees Limited
– director) – Chairman
E Smith (representing Specialist Co Secs Limited – secretary and representing Specialist Co Nominees Limited – director) (being a quorum)

CHAIRMAN

1. IT WAS RESOLVED THAT H. Jones be appointed as Chairman of the Meeting.

BOARD CHANGES:

2. IT WAS RESOLVED THAT with effect from the end of the meeting the resignation of Specialist Co Nominees Limited as company director be and is hereby accepted and that Rupert Max Dashwood be appointed as director in its place.

3. IT WAS RESOLVED THAT with effect from the end of the meeting the resignation of Specialist Co Secs Limited as secretary be and is hereby accepted and that Fiona Dashwood be appointed as secretary in its place.

TRANSFER OF SHARES

4. IT WAS RESOLVED THAT the following stamped transfers relating to the subscribers' shares be approved in accordance with the articles of association:

Number of Transfer	Transferor	Transferee	Number of ord. shares of £1
1	Specialist Co Nominees Limited	Rupert Max Dashwood	one
2	Specialist Co Secs Limited	Fiona Dashwood	one

5. IT WAS RESOLVED THAT the Secretary be instructed to register the above transfers in the books of the Company and in due course issue share certificates to the transferees.

CHANGE OF REGISTERED OFFICE:

6. IT WAS RESOLVED THAT the registered office address of the company be and is hereby changed to: Felix House, Dogget Road, Chatham, Kent.

CLOSURE

7. There being no further business, the Chairman closed the meeting.

_____

CHAIRMAN:

Figure 4.2 Sample first board minutes approving appointment of new director, secretary, transfer of subscribers' shares and change of registered office address

To: the Board of Directors   Date: 6/4/03
Dashwood & Sons Limited,

Dear Sirs,

We hereby give our resignation as company director and waive all claims for compensation or loss of fees for loss of office or otherwise.

Yours faithfully,

Specialist Co Nominees Limited

To: the Board of Directors   Date: 6/4/03
Dashwood & Sons Limited,

Dear Sirs,

We hereby tender our resignation as company secretary and waive all claims for compensation or loss of fees for loss of office or otherwise.

Yours faithfully,

Specialist Co Secs Limited

Figure 4.3   Letters of resignation from first director and secretary

the legislation that came into force on 2 April 2002, Companies (Particulars of Usual Residential Address) (Confidentiality Orders) Regulations 2002, company officers can apply to the Secretary of State for permission to not disclose their home address. Each application is reviewed by the Secretary of State, and supporting evidence is required such as details of any attack and the police incident number. When the Secretary of State is satisfied that there is a risk then the director is allowed to disclose his address to the Registrar and to publish a service address at Companies House. The form used for Confidentiality Orders is also valid if the Companies House form is used with the barcode as provided. Certain business activities are automatically suitable for Confidentiality Orders and you can check at Companies House for eligibility. Applications are made on Form 723B and submitted with the appropriate fee of £100. Applications need to be sent to the Administrator at PO Box 4082, Cardiff CF14 3WE.

E-filing

In order to protect users of electronic filing, you need to complete the security measure that Companies House requires to protect the information. Before you can use WebFiling you will need to apply for a security code. This code is returned to you electronically. You will also need to obtain a Company Authentication code for each of the companies on whose behalf you are filing documents. This can be obtained via the WebFiling Service. The following documents can currently be filed electronically: *Change of Registered Office (287)*; *Appointment of a Director or Secretary (288a)*; *Termination of a Director or Secretary (288b)*; *Changes to a Director or Secretary's Details (288c)*; *Allotment of Shares (88(2)* and *88(3))*; *Increase in Nominal Capital and Resolution (123)*; *Location of the Register of Members (353)*; *Location of Debenture Holders (190);* and, *The Annual Return (363)*.

Companies House
— *for the record* —

Please complete in typescript,
or in bold black capitals.

CHFP000

288a

APPOINTMENT of director or secretary
(NOT for resignation (use Form 288b) or change
of particulars (use Form 288c))

Company Number	000145567

Company Name in full	DASHWOOD & SONS LIMITED

	Day	Month	Year		Day	Month	Year
Date of appointment	0 6	0 4	2 0 0 3	†Date of Birth	0 4	0 4	1 9 6 4

Appointment form

Notes on completion appear on reverse.

Appointment as director [X]   as secretary [ ]   *Please mark the appropriate box. If appointment is as a director and secretary mark both boxes.*

NAME	*Style / Title	MR	*Honours etc	✓

	Forename(s)	RUPERT MAX

	Surname	DASHWOOD

	Previous Forename(s)	✓	Previous Surname(s)	✓

†† Tick this box if the address shown is a service address for the beneficiary of a Confidentiality Order granted under the provisions of section 723B of the Companies Act 1985 [ ]

†† Usual residential address	GREENFIELDS, 14 WALKER CLOSE

Post town	CHATHAM	Postcode	KE1 4EP

County / Region	KENT	Country	U.K

†Nationality	BRITISH	†Business occupation	SALES MANAGER

†Other directorships (additional space overleaf)	NONE

I consent to act as ** director / secretary of the above named company

Consent signature — *R. M. Dashwood*   Date *6 April 2003*

* Voluntary details.
† Directors only.
**Delete as appropriate

A director, secretary etc must sign the form below.

Signed — *Fiona Dashwood*   Date *6 April 2003*

(**a director / secretary / administrator / administrative receiver / receiver manager / receiver)

You do not have to give any contact information in the box opposite but if you do, it will help Companies House to contact you if there is a query on the form. The contact information that you give will be visible to searchers of the public record..

DASHWOOD + SONS LIMITED, FELIX HOUSE
DOGGET ROAD, CHATHAM, KENT
KE1 4EP   Tel 01233-7270000
DX number ___ DX exchange ___

Companies House receipt date barcode

This form has been provided free of charge by Companies House

When you have completed and signed the form please send it to the Registrar of Companies at:
Companies House, Crown Way, Cardiff, CF14 3UZ   DX 33050 Cardiff
for companies registered in England and Wales   **or**
Companies House, 37 Castle Terrace, Edinburgh, EH1 2EB
for companies registered in Scotland   **DX 235 Edinburgh**

Form April 2002

Company Number 000 145567

† Directors only.

†Other directorships NONE

NOTES

Show the full forenames, NOT INITIALS. If the director or secretary is a corporation or Scottish firm, show the name on surname line and registered or principal office on the usual residential line.

Give previous forenames or surname(s) except:
- for a married woman, the name by which she was known before marriage need not be given.
- for names not used since the age of 18 or for at least 20 years

A peer or individual known by a title may state the title instead of or in addition to the forenames and surname and need not give the name by which that person was known before he or she adopted the title or succeeded to it.

Other directorships.

Give the name of every company incorporated in Great Britain of which the person concerned is a director or has been a director at any time in the past five years.

You may exclude a company which either is, or at all times during the past five years when the person concerned was a director, was
- dormant
- a parent company which wholly owned the company making the return, or
- another wholly owned subsidiary of the same parent company.

Companies House
—— *for the record* ——

*Please complete in typescript,
or in bold black capitals.*

CHFP000

288a

APPOINTMENT of director or secretary
(NOT for resignation (use Form 288b) or change of particulars (use Form 288c))

Company Number | `000145567`

Company Name in full | `DASHWOOD & SONS LIMITED`

	Day	Month	Year		Day	Month	Year
Date of appointment	`0 6`	`0 4`	`2 0 0 3`	**†Date of Birth**			

Appointment form

Notes on completion appear on reverse.

Appointment as director [ ]   as secretary [X]   *Please mark the appropriate box. If appointment is as a director and secretary mark both boxes.*

NAME   *Style / Title* [ ]   *Honours etc* [ ]

Forename(s) `FIONA`

Surname `DASHWOOD`

Previous Forename(s) [ ]   *Previous Surname(s)* [ ]

†† Tick this box if the address shown is a service address for the beneficiary of a Confidentiality Order granted under the provisions of section 723B of the Companies Act 1985 [ ]

†† **Usual residential address** `GREEN FIELDS, 14 WALKER CLOSE`

Post town `CHATHAM`   *Postcode* `KE1 6EP`

County / Region `KENT`   *Country* [ ]

†*Nationality* [ ]   †*Business occupation* [ ]

†*Other directorships* (additional space overleaf) [ ]

I consent to act as ** director / secretary of the above named company

Consent signature `Fiona Dashwood`   **Date** `6 April 2003`

* Voluntary details.
† Directors only.
**Delete as appropriate

A director, secretary etc must sign the form below.

Signed `R. M Dashwood`   **Date** `6 April 2003`

(**a director / secretary / administrator / administrative receiver / receiver manager / receiver)

You do not have to give any contact information in the box opposite but if you do, it will help Companies House to contact you if there is a query on the form. The contact information that you give will be visible to searchers of the public record..

`DASHWOOD & SONS LIMITED`
`FELIX HOUSE, DOGGET ROAD, CHATHAM`
`KENT KE1 4EP`   Tel `01233 - 7370000`

DX number [ ]   DX exchange [ ]

Companies House receipt date barcode

This form has been provided free of charge by Companies House

Form April 2002

When you have completed and signed the form please send it to the Registrar of Companies at:
Companies House, Crown Way, Cardiff, CF14 3UZ   DX 33050 Cardiff
for companies registered in England and Wales   **or**
Companies House, 37 Castle Terrace, Edinburgh, EH1 2EB
for companies registered in Scotland   **DX 235 Edinburgh**

Company Number 000145567

† Directors only.

†Other directorships N/A

NOTES
Show the full forenames, NOT INITIALS. If the director or secretary is a corporation or Scottish firm, show the name on surname line and registered or principal office on the usual residential line.

Give previous forenames or surname(s) except:
 - for a married woman, the name by which she was known before marriage need not be given.
 - for names not used since the age of 18 or for at least 20 years
A peer or individual known by a title may state the title instead of or in addition to the forenames and surname and need not give the name by which that person was known before he or she adopted the title or succeeded to it.

Other directorships.
Give the name of every company incorporated in Great Britain of which the person concerned is a director or has been a director at any time in the past five years.

You may exclude a company which either is, or at all times during the past five years when the person concerned was a director, was
 - dormant
 - a parent company which wholly owned the company making the return, or
 - another wholly owned subsidiary of the same parent company.

Companies House
— *for the record* —

Please complete in typescript, or in bold black capitals.
CHFP000

288b

Terminating appointment as director or secretary
(NOT for appointment (use Form 288a) or change of particulars (use Form 288c))

Company Number | 000145567

Company Name in full | DASHWOOD & SONS LIMITED

	Day	Month	Year
Date of termination of appointment	06	04	20 0 3

as director [ ]   as secretary [ ]

Please mark the appropriate box. If terminating appointment as a director and secretary mark both boxes.

NAME

Please insert details as previously notified to Companies House.

*Style / Title [ ]   *Honours etc [ ]

Forename(s) [ ]

Surname | SPECIALIST Co NOMINEES LIMITED

	Day	Month	Year
†Date of Birth			

A serving director, secretary etc must sign the form below.

Signed | R M Dashwood | **Date** | 6 April 2003

* Voluntary details.
† Directors only.
** Delete as appropriate

(** serving director / secretary / administrator / administrative receiver / receiver manager / receiver)

You do not have to give any contact information in the box opposite but if you do, it will help Companies House to contact you if there is a query on the form. The contact information that you give will be visible to searchers of the public record.

DASHWOOD & SONS LIMITED, FELIX HOUSE
DOGGET ROAD, CHATHAM, KENT
KE1 4EP   Tel 01233 - 7270000

DX number   DX exchange

Companies House receipt date barcode

This form has been provided free of charge by Companies House.

10/03

When you have completed and signed the form please send it to the Registrar of Companies at:
Companies House, Crown Way, Cardiff, CF14 3UZ   **DX 33050 Cardiff**
for companies registered in England and Wales   **or**
Companies House, 37 Castle Terrace, Edinburgh, EH1 2EB   **DX 235 Edinburgh**
for companies registered in Scotland   **or LP - 4 Edinburgh 2**

Table 4.4 Checklist for the appointment of a company director

Action	✓
Procedure for appointment of first directors on incorporation	
1. First company director(s) appointed on *Form 10* (see page 116) and delivered to Companies House with other registration documents (*Form 12*, Memorandum and Articles of Association) together with registration fee. If you buy a shelf company, this will already have been dealt with by the agents. – director(s) and secretary to sign form – form countersigned by subscribers or agents	
2. Details of first company director(s) to be entered into the company registers (register of directors and secretaries/register of directors' interests), after incorporation – appointment effective from incorporation – ask director to disclose interests in contracts	
3. Company director(s) to sign bank mandate on opening a new bank account – supply specimen signatures	
4. Prepare service contract (if appropriate)	
5. Give each director a copy of the Memorandum and Articles of Association (accepted good company secretarial practice), advise future board meeting dates	
6. Issue company credit cards, company car etc (see (5), below)	
Procedure for appointment of subsequent company directors (when purchasing an off-the-shelf company follow *)	
1. Approval of resignation/appointment of director by the board * – hold a meeting of directors to approve the change * – minute decisions	
2. Send notice of resignation/appointment to Companies House * (*Forms 288a* and *288b)* within 14 days. Advise other relevant organizations, eg Stock Exchange (listed companies)	
3. Complete details of the resignation/appointment in the register of directors * and secretaries and complete register of directors' interests, where relevant	
4. Amend bank mandate – forward specimen signature(s) to bank if the appointee is to be a bank signatory	

Table 4.4 continued

	Action	✓
5.	General administrative matters:	
*	– give appointee a copy of the Memorandum and Articles of Association	
*	– issue new service contract, if required	
*	– credit card	
*	– fleet car	
*	– PAYE matters	
	– check directors' indemnity policy covers new appointee	
*	– check/amend headed notepaper, if necessary	
*	– deal with share qualification, where appropriate	
*	– disclosure of directors' interests in shares or contracts	
6.	Advise customers, suppliers and other relevant organizations (eg auditors, Inland Revenue, regulatory bodies) of the appointment	
7.	Listed plcs will have additional notification requirements, eg press release (they should notify the Stock Exchange)	

Where a director is interested in shares in the company and/or group companies he or she must complete a notice about this interest and pass it to the company secretary. Upon receipt of the notice, the company secretary needs to make the relevant entry into the register of directors' interests. This register must be open to inspection by the shareholders and members of the public.

A director is obliged to notify the company in writing of any of the following events:

1. Any event which results in him or her becoming interested/ceasing to be interested in shares or debentures of the company or any other company within the group.
2. Any contract entered into by the director to sell any such shares or debentures.
3. Assignment by him or her of a right granted to subscribe for shares or debentures in the company.
4. The grant to the director by another company in the group of a right to subscribe for shares or debentures in that other company and the exercise of any right granted or assignment by him or her of the right.

An example of a standard form of notification is given in Figure 4.4.

Notice by Director of Interest in Shares (Companies Act 1985 s324)

To: The Directors
       Dashwood & Sons Limited
       Felix House
       Dogget Road
       Chatham
       Kent

I HEREBY NOTIFY you in fulfilment of the obligation imposed by the Companies Act 1985 s324 that I have become interested in Shares in the Company.

Date of acquiring: 30.4.03

Nature of Interest: Beneficial Ownership

Number and Class of Shares involved: 1500 Ordinary £1.00 Shares

Please record the above particulars in the Register maintained by you pursuant to Companies Act 1985 s325 and acknowledge receipt of this notice.

Yours faithfully,

R M DASHWOOD

DATE:

Figure 4.4   Draft notice of a director's interest

Restrictions on appointment of directors

Certain people are prevented by law from being appointed as directors. You should check the Articles of Association for any special regulations that may apply specifically to your company to stop certain people being appointed. The Articles may, for example, stipulate that each director must hold a certain number of shares in the company. In general, the following people cannot, by law, be appointed as directors:

- a person disqualified from being a director by any provision of the Act or by a court order;

- undischarged bankrupts (unless authorized by the court);
- the auditor of the company;
- a person suffering from a mental disorder.

Note. Companies legislation contains various provisions under which directors are disqualified automatically, or by court order. The Articles of a company may make provision for disqualification or automatic retirement. Failure by a director to attend board meetings for six months or more without the consent of the board can leave him or her open to removal unless Table A has been altered. Directors of public companies and their subsidiaries are required by the Companies Act to retire at the age of 70, although they can be reappointed annually with the shareholders' approval.

Directors' duties

Directors owe certain duties to their company. These include duties of care and skill, statutory duties and fiduciary duties. Directors may be liable to their company for negligence although the courts are usually reluctant to interfere with business decisions. Statutory duties will normally be performed on behalf of the company but the secretary and directors are also liable in cases of default. There is also a duty to keep minutes of board meetings and to file accounts.

Fiduciary duties include: the avoidance of a conflict of interest; the avoidance of making secret profits; and the obligation to run the company for the benefit of the company as a whole. In short, the fiduciary responsibility of a director is to act for the company's benefit and in the best interest of the shareholders. The office of director should not be used to make personal profits. Directors must also act in the interest of the company's employees.

You should note that directors will need to disclose any matters which might influence their dealings with the company, or any interest in a contract (or proposed contract) with the company. In deciding what constitutes an interest, you should interpret the term 'directors' to include shadow directors and spouses, children, trustees, and other connected persons. Be aware that conflicts of interest can arise from the following: contracts of employment; loans; and property transactions.

A director's interests in other companies should also be notified to the secretary who can then ensure disclosure is made to the board as necessary. Directors are under an obligation to ensure disclosure is made, and should do so to protect themselves from any claim that they have made a secret profit from a transaction. Otherwise the company can claw back all secret profits and declare the contract void.

Director: protection from liability

The Companies (Audit, Investigations and Community Enterprise) Act 2004, introduced from 6 April 2005 allowed companies to provide greater protection to the director from liability. In particular, companies can provide funds to meet the cost of defending actions brought against the directors. It allows the company to assist with costs to defend proceedings, which in the past could only be paid after there was a judgement in favour of the director. It also recognized that directors were facing increasing litigation from third parties, particularly in the US. Whilst this allows payment for some defence costs, certain actions for defence are precluded eg criminal negligence.

Contracts of employment for directors

Often, a director is employed under a service contract which details remuneration and conditions of employment. The company secretary should ensure that the directors' service contracts or a memorandum of its terms (when there is no written contract) are available for inspection by any shareholder. These documents are usually kept at the registered office address. When service contracts are not kept at the registered office, the secretary must notify Companies House on *Form 318* (see page 133) of the address at which they are kept.

There are statutory controls preventing directors abusing their powers by awarding themselves long-term service contracts which are not in the interests of their company. Table 4.5 gives a checklist for directors' service contracts.

Table 4.5 Checklist for directors' service contracts

Action	✓
Set up a record of directors' service contracts	
If directors' service contracts are stored at a place other than the registered office address, file completed *Form 318* at Companies House	
Approval for contracts over five years in length by an ordinary resolution of the members	
(**NB.** The *Committee on Corporate Governance, The Combined Code,* recommends that contract periods should be for one year or less.)	

Directors' remuneration

Where a director is an employee of the company under a contract of service (whether in writing, or not) remuneration will be governed by the terms of the contract. It is normal for the company's Articles of Association to provide for directors' fees to be paid, such fees being distinct from the remuneration paid to an executive director under a service contract. You need to ensure that the company's Articles of Association permit the remuneration of directors as there is not an automatic right. The company's Articles of Association should also confirm the process for the approval of remuneration. There is no automatic right for remuneration of alternate directors unless this is stated in the company's Articles of Association.

Certain companies are required to establish a Remuneration committee to make recommendations for directors'. Recommendations from remuneration committees need to consider benchmarking and market conditions, the time needed to fulfil the role and that consideration be given to the pay situation elsewhere in the company.

Full disclosure of all fees and benefits, received by directors from their role as an officer, must be in the notes to the company's annual accounts, under the Directors Remuneration Report Regulations 2002.

Insolvency

A director may be held personally liable when a company trades while insolvent, ie it cannot meet its obligations or pay its debts. He or she may be required to make such contribution (if any) to the company's assets as the court thinks proper if, in the course of the winding up, it appears that any business of the company was carried out with the intent to defraud its creditors (fraudulent trading). This also applies (for wrongful trading) if, in the course of the winding up, it appears that:

1. the company has gone into insolvent liquidation;
2. at some time before the winding up, the director knew (or should have known) that there was no reasonable prospect that the company would avoid going into insolvent liquidation;
3. the director did not take every step to minimize the potential loss to the company's creditors;
4. they were a director at the time.

Directors should be aware that a company may be deemed to be insolvent when its liabilities exceed its assets. Professional advice should be sought quickly from the company's accountants in these circumstances, in order to limit any personal liability.

Loans

In general, for most private companies, loans or guarantees to directors are prohibited, except in limited circumstances. The Companies Act 1985 contains complex provisions governing loans and similar transactions. It is possible that the company's Articles of Association may place further restrictions on the directors. Expenses that are incurred on business for the company can be repaid. One of the main intentions of the restrictions in the Companies Act is to prohibit tax-free sums being paid to directors by the company.

Very simply, loans in excess of £5,000 (in aggregate) are prohibited (s 334 CA 1985). However, there is no repayment period given for a small loan of up to £5,000. Short-term quasi-loans for credit and charge cards can be for an aggregate amount of up to £5,000, but repayment is required within two months. The amount of a quasi-loan for a public company or a subsidiary of a plc, or has a plc as a subsidiary or it is a subsidiary of a company which has another subsidiary as a plc ('relevant company') is higher (£10,000). Advance payments for expenses will need to be approved at a general meeting, ie for legitimate business expenditure. If the expenses are not approved, the funds must be repaid in six months. Plcs or relevant companies must not make payments greater than £20,000 for expenses incurred (s337). The amount available is periodically updated and you should check the relevant legislation. Banks and some other types of lending company are exempted from certain restrictions (for example, they can give mortgages at a favourable rate). Directors should be mindful that they must disclose details of loans in the company accounts.

Following events in the United States, the Sarbanes–Oxley Act 2002 has amended the US Securities Exchange Act 1934, and it now prohibits companies from extending credit such as personal loans to directors and officers. Company secretaries of UK companies need to be aware that these US regulations may affect their UK group if their shares are listed on a US stock exchange or shares are traded in the United States. This also applies if the company is part of a US group or a UK group with US obligations.

The regulations on directors loans have been amended so that funds can be advanced to a director to allow him or her to defend criminal proceedings or applications for relief. If the director is convicted, or relief refused, any funds advanced must be returned.

Substantial property transactions

Companies are subject to restrictions to prevent them from transferring assets from or to directors of the company or its holding company. An asset covered by this rule (s 320 CA 1985) will need shareholder approval if it is worth not more than £2,000, and subject to that, exceeds the lesser of £100,000 or 10 per cent of the company's asset value and is not between companies in a wholly owned group. Any substantial transaction that falls within the definition of s 320 of the Companies Act 1985 can only be effected if the director discloses his or her interest at a board meeting and it is approved by an ordinary resolution at a general meeting of the company. In addition, quoted companies are subjected to the related party transaction restrictions in the Listing Rules. The Companies Act also restricts option dealing for directors of public listed companies (s 323 CA 1985).

There are some exceptions to this rule; if assets are transferred between a trading company and a 100 per cent owned subsidiary, if the transaction is entered into by a company being wound up but not in a members' voluntary liquidation, if the transaction takes place on a recognised investment exchange, or it is in relation to a member who is acquiring the asset as a shareholder (note the dividend in specie must be treated carefully).

Types of director

The duties and responsibilities of a director can attach to any individual who occupies the position of director whatever the name or title by which they are known.

- **Chairman of the board of directors**. He or she will take the chair at board meetings and general meetings. It is the chairman's role to act as the leader of the board and he or she may be called upon to settle questions of policy or decisions affecting the company. This role of arbitrator is often reflected in the company's Articles of Association by giving the chairman the casting vote on board resolutions.
- **Managing director**. He or she has no specific powers accorded to him or her by law: authority is based entirely in the terms of the delegation by the board and his or her service contract (if any). Responsibilities will vary greatly in practice but usually he or she has overall charge of the running of the company. The board may delegate to any managing director the powers that they consider necessary if they have been authorized to do so in the Articles of Association.
- **Non-executive directors.** These types of director are part time and are usually appointed because of their specialist knowledge and commercial experience. They are not involved in day-to-day management and are appointed for the knowledge that they bring to board meetings. They usually have no involvement in the day-to-day management of the company. However, non-executive directors have fiduciary and other duties to the company and have a duty to use care and skill in carrying out their role.

- **Directors in name only**. This type of appointment can be referred to as **associate, assistant, local** or **special** director. These titles are usually used to enhance the status of employees when they are dealing with outside contacts, and are not designed to confirm appointment as directors under the Companies Acts. It is generally considered bad practice to hold people out to be directors unless appointed as such. It can lead to confusion and give rise to other problems both for the company and the individual concerned. The company could be bound by any resulting contracts. These titles should only be used if it is clearly stated in the company's Articles of Association that these types of directors are **not** members of the board.
- **Shadow directors**. This is the title given to people who have not been appointed as directors, but control other directors. Appointment as director may be effective even though the paperwork has not been completed! Thus, a director is to be recognized by his or her function.
- **Alternate directors**. They are appointed, for example, to take the place of a director when abroad or otherwise unavailable. They have the same legal duties as other directors and are appointed, if permitted by the Articles, following a board resolution and by giving notice to Companies House.

Company secretary

Every company must have a secretary who is not also the sole director. The company secretary is usually appointed by the board of directors. The details of the appointment of the first secretary are given on *Form 10* (see page 116) which is filed at Companies House when the application for the incorporation of the company is made. The first secretary will give on this form their full name and address and sign it to consent to act as secretary. Of course, if your company is purchased off the shelf, these details have already been filed at Companies House and the first secretary has already been appointed. As a result, when you buy your shelf company, you will be asked to arrange for the new appointee. A *Form 288a* (page 129) should be completed to give notice of the appointment of the new secretary and a *Form 288b* (page 131) for the resignation of the old one. You will also find, when you purchase a shelf company, that the documents supplied include a letter of resignation from the old secretary together with the board minutes approving this change. If these minutes have not been supplied, you should draft a set of minutes using the example given on page 37.

The notice of an appointment of one person as a director and secretary can be sent to Companies House on the same document *(Form 288a)*.

It is important that a copy of this (and any other) form filed at Companies House be kept with the statutory records. They can then be referred to when completing the company registers (see Chapter 6).

The company secretary is usually responsible for compliance matters. In the context of a small company this amounts to maintaining the statutory books and records recording board decisions, insurance matters, as well as a plethora of other details ranging from PAYE to car fleet management. Unfortunately, company secretaries do tend to have any extraneous matters dumped upon them – so beware. Because of the range and breadth of the job, it is difficult to include all of the areas that may be included in a job profile. However, it is possible to distil the core areas of the role of secretary in a small company, or in a larger company, by their company secretarial departments.

The core areas include the following:

- maintaining the statutory books;
- attending board and general meetings and taking minutes;
- dealing with insurance policies;
- ensuring good corporate governance.

See Chapter 1 for a summary of the duties of a company secretary.

It should be noted that a company secretary is defined by the Companies Act as being an officer of the company which means that they may be liable for fines and penalties for breaches of the Act. The position should not be taken lightly as the penalties now levied can be substantial. As an officer of the company the secretary owes fiduciary duties to the company similar to those owed by a director. No provision in the company's Articles or otherwise which purports to exempt the secretary from liability in respect of negligence, default, breach of duty or trust can be enforced. As with the directors, the secretary should always take care, when making contracts, to ensure that he or she does so as the company's agent if personal liability is to be avoided.

Table 4.6 Checklist for the appointment of a company secretary

Action	✓
Procedure for appointment of first company secretary on incorporation	
1. First company secretary appointed on *Form 10* (see page 000), delivered to Companies House with other registration documents. If you buy an off-the-shelf company, this will already have been dealt with by the agents. – secretary signs form – form countersigned by subscribers or the agent for the subscriber	
2. Details of first company secretary to be entered into the company registers (register of directors and secretaries) – appointment effective from incorporation	
3. Company secretary to sign bank mandate on opening a new bank account	
4. Prepare service contract if appropriate (fleet car, credit cards, etc)	
Note. Consider if you need to complete a confidentiality order to use a service address on the public records	
Procedure for appointment of subsequent company secretaries (follow * for shelf companies)	
1. Approval of resignation of the original (unless appointing additional 'joint' secretary) and appointment of new secretary by the board of directors * – hold a meeting of directors to approve the change * – minute decisions	
2. Send notice of resignation/appointment to Companies House * *(Forms 288b* and *288a,* pages 131 and 129) within 14 days	
3. Complete details of the resignation/appointment in the register of * directors and secretaries	
4. Amend bank mandate if secretary is signatory on the company's * bank account – forward specimen signature to bank	
5. Advise relevant organizations (auditors, solicitors, etc) *	
6. Press release/advise customers and suppliers *	
7. For listed public companies there are additional rules that apply, eg notify the Stock Exchange	
Note. Consider if you need to complete a form for a confidentiality order to use a service address on the public records	

The first allotments – subscriber shares

The first shares issued by a company on incorporation are known as subscriber shares. In the case of a company purchased off the shelf, it is normal for two shares to be issued (although only one share now needs to be issued if it is a private company). The applicants for these shares will have their names and addresses printed on the last pages of the company's Memorandum and Articles of Association.

Following the acquisition of a shelf company, transfer of the two subscriber shares will have to be approved at the company's first board meeting. Details concerning the share transfer must then be recorded in the company's register of transfers and members.

If you form your own company, the subscriber shares can be allotted to shareholders of your choice from the beginning. You will still need to ensure that the shares are paid for (if appropriate) and that details are entered in the register of allotments and in the register of members.

Opening a bank account

The directors of a company will need to decide which bank to use for their company account(s). It is worth exploring the range of facilities on offer from competing banks before making a decision. Once a bank and branch have been chosen, you will be asked to complete a **bank mandate form**, and specimen signature card. The type of form provided may vary. The form will set out a resolution that the bank will require the board of directors to pass to authorize the opening of an account. You will also need to comply with the bank requirements for identification evidence to the company.

The minutes of the meeting which records the appointment of bankers will need to note its approval of the resolutions in the bank mandate form. The chairman of the meeting and the company secretary will usually be required to sign the bank mandate form. The signatories to the bank account will need to sign the specimen signature section (these do not have to be the same officers as those who sign the bank mandate). It is possible that two, or more, specimen signatures will be required from each signatory.

Selecting an accounting reference date

Every company has to have an accounting reference date (ARD). This is the date in each calendar year which determines the end of its accounting reference period (ARP), for example 31 March. In this case the company will present its accounts to the 31 March in each successive year. A company's first ARP may not be for a period shorter than six months, according to statute, however in practice shorter periods than six months may be accepted by Companies House. It is advisable to obtain authority in writing if you wish to do this. No ARP may exceed a period of 18 months. The first ARP of a company runs from the date of incorporation to its chosen ARD.

You must give notification of your chosen ARD on *Form 225* (see page 127) to Companies House within nine months of the date of incorporation. If you fail to file this form, you will automatically be allocated an ARD which is the last day of the month following the anniversary of when the company was incorporated (eg a company incorporated 15 June would be automatically given the date of 30 June as its year end if it fails to give notice of its chosen ARD).

It is important to ensure that the company's accounts are made up to within seven days either side of the ARD registered at Companies House. (Note that one cannot extend an 18-month period by a further seven days.) Accounts made up to the wrong ARD will automatically be rejected. This could prove costly and inconvenient since accounts would have to be prepared to the date determined by the Registrar, and they may be late, in which case the company may be subject to an automatic late filing penalty. The resolution to approve the company's ARD must be passed by the board of directors and be recorded in the minutes.

A company may change its ARD during its **current** period or alter the previous period by filing *Form 225* (see page 127). A company may shorten or extend its ARP and give details of the new ARD. A company may only extend its ARP (not exceeding 18 months) once every five years, with the following exceptions:

1. the company is parent/subsidiary of another company incorporated in the European Economic Area (EEA, which comprises the EU countries plus Liechtenstein, Iceland and Norway) – in this case the ARDs must be the same **and** be one of the original dates, subject to the 18-month rule;

2. when the company is subject to an administration order;
3. when permitted by the Secretary of State.

The deadline for filing the *Form 225* to alter the current period is when that period expires. When altering a previous period, the *Form 225* must be filed within the time allowed for filing accounts for the previous accounting period (for example, within the ten months allowed for private companies).

Choosing an auditor

Every company must have an auditor with the exception of:

- dormant companies;
- audit exempt companies.

The company's first auditors are appointed by a resolution of the board of directors. The auditors will then remain in office until the first general meeting of the company at which accounts are presented. At this meeting, the current auditors can be reappointed or others may be appointed to replace them.

Note that certain categories of company that meet the criteria of being a 'small company' under the Companies Act may be exempt from the requirements to have their accounts audited.

5

Corporate governance and day-to-day administration

The company secretary is responsible for the day-to-day administration of a company and this will include ensuring that the regulations governing board meetings are met. Duties will also include keeping the minutes, making the necessary entries in the statutory books and notifying Companies House of changes.

Board meetings

Except to the extent that the whole or any part of the powers of the board have been delegated to a single director, or the Articles provide for written resolutions signed by all directors, the directors must act through resolutions taken either at board meetings or committees of the board to whom a matter may have been referred. The convening of and proceedings of a board are, in consequence, of prime importance in the proper management of the company. The Combined Code June 2004 which applies to listed plc's requires boards to meet sufficiently regularly to discharge their duties effectively. Boards must also establish a formal list of matters that are reserved for decision by the board of directors.

Formal meetings are held by directors as a board in order to approve business matters. It is an advantage for the company directors to meet as a board when there are some directors who may not be involved in the running of the business (for example, non-executive directors). Larger companies will commonly hold meetings regularly (say, monthly) so that a yearly timetable can be given to all directors. When meetings of directors have not already been set, the chairman will ask the secretary to convene a meeting. There is no length of notice set by statute, the period simply needs to be reasonable bearing in mind the practice of the company and other related circumstances. If the directors can all be contacted easily at short notice then, in theory, notice of a few hours or minutes would be sufficient. However, the length of notice given should give all the company's directors a reasonable opportunity to attend the meeting. All the directors must be given notice because business conducted at a meeting of which only some of the directors have notice is invalid. Notice does not have to be in writing.

You will need to check the company's Articles of Association for any special rules that may apply to the calling of board meetings. If there are no extra provisions, board meetings may be held when appropriate. In theory, a company must hold at least one meeting of the board a year in order to approve the company's accounts, and to authorize the calling of the annual general meeting. However, in most companies business matters intervene and meetings are held more frequently.

Business may be delegated to a sub committee of the board for a single project such as an aquisition or for an ongoing purpose, eg Remuneration committee, Nomination committee or an Audit committee.

Quorum

The company's Articles will usually specify the number of directors required to form a quorum at board meetings. This is the minimum number of people required to be present for the meeting to be valid. Where the company has a sole director (provided this is permitted by the Articles) he or she shall have authority to exercise all the powers and directions vested in the directors generally. Decisions of the sole director need to be recorded in writing (see *Written resolutions* on page 65). If the number of directors falls to below the prescribed minimum in the Articles, the continuing director may act solely but only for the purpose of increasing the number of directors to the minimum (or for calling a general meeting).

Chairman

In Table A (see page 27), the directors are permitted to appoint a chairman of the board and may, at any time, remove him or her from that office. This should not be confused with removing that person in his or her capacity as a director. The removal of directors is a separate issue (see page 98). The person elected as chairman will chair board and general meetings of the company. If no director is appointed as chairman, the directors may appoint one of their number to chair each meeting at the beginning of the meeting.

Dashwood & Sons Limited

Agenda for Board Meeting to be held on 17 April 2003 at
Felix House, Dogget Road, Chatham, Kent at 09.30 am

AGENDA

1. Chairman's opening remarks
2. To note and approve
    2.1 Certificate of Incorporation
    2.2 appointment of director
    2.3 appointment of secretary
    2.4 registered office address
3. Approval of share transfers
4. Allotment of shares
5. Approval of accounting reference date
6. Appointment of auditors
7. Appointment of bankers
8. Adoption of company seal
9. Disclosure of directors' interests in shares and contracts
10. Any other business
11. Date of next meeting

Figure 5.1   Sample agenda of a board meeting

The agenda

The business to be discussed at a board meeting is set out in an agenda. Items of business are numbered consecutively to assist minute taking and referencing. A draft agenda for the first board meeting of Dashwood & Sons Limited is shown in Figure 5.1.

Preparing for a meeting

The company secretary is responsible for organizing meetings and Table 5.1 is a checklist of the procedure.

Table 5.1   Preparation checklist for board meetings

	Action	✓
1.	Prepare a notice of the board meeting when instructed by the directors (include date, time, venue and agenda) and draft proposed resolutions. Check that the chair has approved the agenda (and ideally, that the rest of the board have been given an opportunity to comment on the draft agenda).	
2.	Send out the notice (and agenda if available) to: – directors – any company managers or professional advisors invited	
3.	Prepare duplicate copies of the agenda, formal resolutions, and reports for the meeting, collate and arrange for copies of any other documents to be considered at the meeting	
4.	Check: – the venue – ensure that the boardroom is prepared – availability of directors – a quorum will be reached	
5.	Take to the meeting: – a copy of the last minutes for signature – a copy of the Memorandum and Articles of Association – the directors' attendance book – the minute book – a copy of the Companies Act – agenda and other necessary documents – in the case of a public company, the register of directors' interests	

The meeting

At the meeting, the secretary must ensure that the directors sign an attendance book if one is maintained. He or she must also ensure that there is a quorum as required by the Articles of Association. At the start of the meeting the secretary should record any apologies for absence. Table 5.2 is a checklist of the duties of the secretary at the meeting. The secretary needs to provide an accurate record of the proceedings. It is important that requests to record, say, a particular director's dissent are followed and the request is clearly noted. This is however exceptional as generally board resolutions are passed by unanimous consent. It is usual to record the key points that underpin the decisions taken.

Table 5.2   Secretarial duties checklist for board meetings

	Action	✓
1.	Record names of directors and others present – arrange for directors' attendance book to be signed (if kept)	
2.	Record apologies for absence	
3.	Check the quorum and ensure it is maintained throughout the meeting *Note.* If any business occurs in which a director has a personal interest, ensure that there will be a quorum not counting that director (check Articles of Association for this rule)	
4.	Take accurate notes and minute decisions made and duties allocated	
5.	Record the late arrival, or early departure, of any director after the meeting has started	
6.	Be prepared to give advice about procedure and the rules and regulations governing board meetings. You may also need to be prepared to provide technical advice on disclosures etc.	
7.	Arrange for invited people to be brought into the meeting as appropriate	
8.	Collect and destroy surplus confidential papers after the meeting	
9.	Comply with any instructions given by the board to file notices at Companies House or with other authorities	

Once the meeting has finished, the company secretary must prepare minutes from the notes taken. It is usual that the first minutes prepared are in draft form. Draft minutes are then made available for comment upon by the directors and, once agreed, a final set will be produced for approval and signature by the chairman at the next meeting. Once approved and signed, the minutes must, by law, be entered in the company's minute book.

The company secretary may be required to notify other personnel of certain decisions taken. A note should be made of items deferred to future meetings as these can be easily overlooked.

Telephone board meetings

If the company's articles permit, the directors can have a board meeting by telephone (or video) conference. The articles will usually state that the meeting is held where the largest number of directors are located together. When preparing for such a meeting, it is important that the company secretary checks that the telephone or video conference facilities work correctly to avoid unnecessary delay.

Written resolutions

A company may be permitted by its Articles of Association to circulate resolutions in writing to all directors for signature in lieu of attendance at a board meeting. Such resolutions, if signed by all the directors, will be as valid as if passed at board meetings – this may be useful in circumstances where a board meeting cannot be held. The written resolution can either be circulated to all directors in turn for signature on one document, or be copied individually to each director, so that there are a number of signed copies. Each resolution should have the date of the signatory as it is effective at the date that the last director signs. The signed copies of the written resolution must be placed in the company's minute book. The resolution(s) will take effect on the date of the last signature on the document(s).

Keeping the minutes

Minutes must be taken of board and general meetings. Approved minutes need to be entered into the company's minute book(s).

It is important that minutes record accurately, and concisely, the business discussed and decisions agreed. Where business decisions have been made which may be considered unusual, you should record the basic reasons behind the decision. Clarity of language is vital, so are dates and amounts which must be recorded accurately.

After the minutes have been formally signed by the chairman at the next meeting, they must be placed in the minute book and not amended in any way. Alterations can only be made thereafter by an amending minute. The signed minutes (by the chairman of the meeting at which proceedings minuted take place or by the chairman of the next following meeting) are evidence, in law, of the proceedings at that meeting. Until the contrary is proved, the minuted meeting is deemed to have been duly held and convened and all appointments made at the meeting, for example of directors, to be valid.

Minute books

Board and general meeting minutes should always be kept separately but a private company in which the directors and shareholders are the same people will often maintain its minute books at the back of its company registers. This is usually a bound book which requires the pages of minutes to be firmly attached.

Where the directors and shareholders are not the same people, or when outside shareholders are involved, it is **essential** that the minutes of board and general meetings should be kept separately or in a loose-leaf register as shareholders only have the right to inspect the minutes of general meetings.

Some companies, usually the larger ones, choose to store their minutes in a loose-leaf binder. If this is the preferred method, the binder should be securely stored in a lockable cabinet or safe to prevent any unauthorized alterations. Lockable loose-leaf binders are available from legal stationers. To aid security, all the pages of the minute book should be numbered so that the removal of pages can be quickly identified.

It is a legal requirement that the minutes of general meetings be kept at the registered office of the company and are made available for inspection by the shareholders for at least two hours on each business day, free of charge. A company is allowed seven days to provide a shareholder with copies of the minutes when requested and there may be a charge for this. Shareholders do not have any statutory right to inspect board minutes.

Statutory books and notices to Companies House

Following a board meeting a company secretary may have to action various statutory events, which may include:

- allotment of shares;
- transfers of shares;
- appointments and resignations of directors;
- appointments and resignations of secretaries;
- change of registered office address;
- notification of accounting reference date;
- appointment of auditors;
- appointment of bankers.

Allotment of shares

The first shares the company allots on incorporation are called the subscriber shares (see Chapter 4). The names and addresses of the subscribers will be shown on the last page of the Memorandum of Association. Details of these shareholders will need to be the first entries in the registers of allotments and members.

There is a series of steps to follow when applications are made for the allotment of shares. The number of shares a company has in its authorized share capital is stated in the company's Memorandum of Association. If the directors wish to allot more shares than stated, the procedure for increasing share capital will first have to be followed. Before proceeding with any allotment, the Articles of Association should be checked for any restrictions. The Companies Act 1985 contains the provision that if new shares are to be allotted, they must be offered first to existing shareholders on the same or better terms in the same proportion as their current shareholding; these are known as **pre-emption rights on allotment**. For example, where a shareholder holds 10 per cent of the issued share capital of the company and a further allotment of shares is proposed, the shareholder must be offered at least enough shares to allow him or her to maintain that 10 per cent share. A private company's Articles can exclude or amend these provisions.

On the basis that the allotment is not subject to pre-emption rights, and is not an offer by a public company, the checklist in Table 5.3 can be used.

When shares are allotted as fully or partly paid otherwise than in cash (under s88(2)(b)(i)CA1985) a copy of the contract (duly signed) must be submitted with a return of allotments. In the past, a certified copy of the contract was sufficient but Companies House has recently updated their procedures to require a signed contract.

The requirement to have the Inland Revenue 'stamp' a contract, or the particulars that a company needs to file when it allows shares as fully or partly paid for a non-cash consideration, has been removed under Regulation 2 of the Stamp Duty and Stamp Duty Land Tax (Consequential Amendments of Enactments) Regulations 2003, SJ 2003/2868. Amended *Forms 88(2)* and *88(3)* (revised 2005) are for use for shares allotted on or after 1 December 2003.

Table 5.3 Basic share allotment checklist for company secretaries where no pre-emption rights apply

Action	✓
1. Application letter – sent by applicant to the company, with cheque	
2. Check directors are authorized to allot *Note.* Authority is required to be renewed every five years by the company in general meeting unless a relevant elective resolution has been passed (which may extend or not limit the period of authority) – refer to Articles of Association	

Action	✓

3. Authorized share capital
- ensure that there are sufficient unissued shares for the allotment
- check that the directors have authority to allot

4. Articles of Association
- check to ensure that there are no pre-emption rights or restrictions
- other relevant organizations – check that the company does not have to adhere to the guidelines of other organizations (eg plcs need to consider the ABI guidelines)

5. Resolution of directors
- letters of application for the allotment have been received
- must be passed, and recorded in the minutes
- secretary instructed to issue certificate
- authority given for use of seal (if appropriate)

6. Check receipt of funds for the allotment

7. Register of allotments
- make necessary entries

8. Register of members
- enter details of new shareholder (if the new shareholder is also a director, disclosure will need to be made in the Register of Directors' Interests)

9. Prepare share certificate
- complete counterfoil and certificate
- seal or add appropriate wording to certificate
- dated and signed by two officers

10. Send certificate to new shareholder, requesting acknowledgement of receipt

11. Give notice to Companies House
- file *Form 88(2)* (see page 118) within one month of allotment
- when shares allotted for consideration other than cash (eg for goods or services) file an original copy of the contract in writing duly stamped by the Inland Revenue or a contract of sale or, in their absence, a *Form 88(3)* (see page 123)

Transfers of shares

Before proceeding with any transfer of shares, the company secretary will have to refer to the Articles of Association. It is quite common for companies to restrict the right to transfer shares so that they cannot be offered to outsiders without first being offered to current members. This is known as a **pre-emption on share transfer**.

The transfer of legal title to shares can only be effected in writing. A share transfer form is usually used for this purpose. There are two main varieties of non-market transfers, one for use by a company transferring its shares, and one for individuals. The procedure is the same in both instances. Stock transfer forms can be purchased from law stationers.

The person who wishes to sell his or her shares is known as the **transferor**, and the purchaser, the **transferee**. A person wishing to transfer his or her shares, or shareholding, must complete and sign a stock transfer form. If the shares being transferred are nil or partly paid, the transferee will also need to sign the stock transfer form. The form consists of the following sections:

1. amount of the consideration;
2. the name of the company whose shares are being transferred;
3. type and number of shares being transferred;
4. transferor's full name and address;
5. signature of transferor(s) and date of signing;
6. transferee's full name and address;
7. where the shares are part paid, or unpaid – signature of transferee(s).

The procedure on transferring shares is as follows:

1. Complete stock transfer form, to be signed and dated by transferor.
2. Send completed form, together with share certificate and any fee (eg including stamp duty – currently 50p per £100 or part £100 of consideration, ie 0.5 per cent) to the company secretary or Registrars who deal with the share transfers of the company. Note that the minimum fixed-rate of duty is £5.

You should be aware that in certain circumstances for share transfers, no duty (or a nominal amount – £5) is payable to the Inland Revenue as stamp duty. You will find on the reverse side of the form lists of categories to which these conditions apply and the appropriate section of the form should be completed and signed when necessary. If in doubt about stamp duty, you should consult your professional advisors or the Inland Revenue Stamp Office.

The procedure for dealing with a share transfer by a company secretary is given in Table 5.4. It is usual practice for the transferor to complete a stock transfer form, leaving the details of the transferee for their completion. The stock transfer form is handed to the transferee in exchange for the consideration. The transferee is responsible for meeting any stamp duty payable. Once stamped, the stock transfer form can be passed to the company secretary for processing.

Table 5.4 Basic share transfer checklist for company secretaries, where no pre-emption rights apply

Action	✓
1. Check the stock transfer form – name given on transfer form should agree with register of members – name on share certificate should agree – address is as expected – ensure the share details are correct and agree with the certificate – where the transferees have a liability, they should also sign	
2. Ensure that the consideration given is 'reasonable'	
3. Check share certificate is an original	
4. Ensure that the appropriate transfer fee has been enclosed (check Articles). This can occur with flat management companies.	
5. The transfer form needs to be stamped by the Inland Revenue to acknowledge that stamp duty has been paid (or in some instances to confirm an exemption from payment) – where there is no consideration or a nominal amount is paid, the declaration on the reverse side of the transfer form needs to have been completed	
6. Register of members, check to ensure there is no legal restraint on the transfer – does the number of shares being transferred agree with the entry in the register of members?	

Table 5.4   continued

Action	✓

7. Partly paid shares
  – ensure amount paid up is correct
  – if remainder should be paid before transfer, ensure it has been	

8. Cancel old share certificate – where the certificate is for more than is being transferred, a balancing certificate must be prepared and sent to transferor	
9. Registration of the transfer and the stock transfer form should be approved by the board of directors – authority is also needed for the use of the company seal, if appropriate	
10. Make the necessary entry in the register of transfers	

11. Make the necessary entry in the register of members
  – close account of transferor
  – open account of transferee, with details of holding	

12. Issue new share certificate – send to transferee or representative	
13. File stock transfer form and cancelled certificate	
14. Forward new certificate to transferee	

The details of the share transfers must be entered in the register of transfers and register of members. Further details are given in Chapter 6.

Appointments and resignations of directors

Entries for board changes (and any change in their particulars) will need to be made in the register of directors and *Forms 288a, b* and/or *c* (see pages 129–132) notifying the changes filed at Companies House. The appointment or resignation of a director must be approved by a board resolution. A checklist for the procedure for the appointment of subsequent directors is given in Chapter 4. You should ensure that all new directors disclose any interests held and that these are entered in the register of directors' interests.

Table A requires a third of all directors to retire by rotation at the annual general meeting. However, this regulation is often disapplied. The Articles of Association will state whether this safeguard exists. Company directors can be disqualified from acting in certain circumstances, see Chapter 4. Under s303 of the Companies Act 1985, the company's shareholders have the power to remove a director by ordinary resolution in a general meeting regardless of any provision of the director's service contract or in the Articles of Association. However, the procedure can be modified in the Articles. It is quite common for wholly owned subsidiaries to have a provision in their Articles whereby the parent company can remove a director. Needless to say, the removal of a director is a serious matter that should be considered very carefully. Indeed, this can be a legal minefield and if a director will not voluntarily go, one should seriously consider seeking professional advice.

Appointments and resignations of company secretaries

Any change of company secretary (or their address) must be recorded in the register of directors and secretaries (or the register of secretaries, if kept separately) and *Forms 288a, b* and/or *c* filed at Companies House. The appointment or resignation of a secretary needs to be approved by a board resolution. A checklist for the procedure for the appointment of subsequent secretaries is given in Chapter 4.

Change of registered office address

Any change of registered office address must be approved by a resolution of the board, and *Form 287* (see page 128), notifying the change filed at Companies House within 14 days. A full discussion of the registered office address and changes to it can be found in Chapter 4.

Notification of accounting reference date

When the date is changed (or initially selected) approval needs to be given by the board, and the appropriate form filed at Companies

House (see Chapter 4). You should note that Companies House now imposes automatic penalties for the late filing of accounts and it will reject financial statements made up to the wrong year end. Companies House publishes a leaflet called *Accounts and Accounting Reference Dates – GBA3* which is available free of charge on its website, www.companieshouse.org.uk

Appointment of auditors and bankers

It is usually a duty of the company secretary to ensure that the appointment or change of professional advisors is dealt with smoothly. Details concerning the appointment of first auditors, and opening bank accounts, are set out in Chapter 4. Companies House publishes a leaflet called *Auditors – GBA4* which is available free of charge.

Corporate governance

Corporate governance needs to be understood by directors in all companies, as it is the way the directors' management of the company is recorded and checked. Their management must be kept in balance to meet the wishes of the shareholders. While the Combined Code must be followed by listed companies, it is good practice and advisory for other businesses to use the Code as a guideline for enhancing good governance.

Matters reserved for the board

The board has a key role in the governance of the company as it is where management decisions are recorded. Not all the decisions of a business are taken at a board meeting. It is usual for a board to delegate authority for decision making, while retaining responsibility. The board needs to be able to delegate responsibility for operational decisions downwards. However, there are certain matters that should not be delegated, such as the company's budgets and capital expenditure beyond budget, strategy and significant contracts. The board will need to draw up a list of matters that are reserved for the board. This list of matters or reserved powers is controlled by the board and needs to be reviewed from time to time. The list of reserved powers needs to be formally adopted by the board, so that the managers of the business can check on their authority levels.

Accurate information

In order to run the business the board needs to be sure it has reliable and accurate accounting and other data. The board has to be satisfied with the information presented. This can be achieved by setting appropriate internal controls. These can be based on verification or audit of internal information. The accounting records must be correct, with appropriate notes to explain the company's financial position. The company must have robust record keeping systems for its accounting records, statutory books and minute books.

Internal controls

There needs to be in place an internal system to ensure that fraud is prevented. It is important that staff are aware there are policies in place to prevent fraud. Internal checks and controls can also be introduced: for example, ensuring that bank accounts have more than one signatory. For larger companies an internal audit function should exists to report on weaknesses. Internal control was covered by the Report of the Turnbull Committee, which examined the requirements of the Combined Code for listed companies. It basically requires companies to establish proper internal controls and risk management. The Combined Code sets out requirements for public listed companies to report on the risks and mechanisms for internal controls. Companies need to assess both current and future risks, and establish mechanisms to control and monitor risk.

Compliance

It is a basic duty to ensure that the company meets its legal obligations, for example to file accounts and annual returns. In complying with the law directors need to act with integrity, follow the laws and avoid anti-competitive behaviours.

E-mail

The rise of e-commerce has brought with it a new series of risks for businesses. From a governance perspective e-mail and computers, while they help companies to do business, are another area of risk. Key legislation exists to regulate the way personal information is held, such as the Data Protection Act, the Human Rights Act 1998 and the Regulation of Investigatory Powers Act 2000. A company needs to ensure that it has the following policies:

- A clear retention of information policy. The regulations set down how long information needs to be stored. A useful booklet on information retention is published by the ICSA.
- Security of data. This can be achieved by using passwords and changing them frequently.

Health and safety

The company has a duty to provide a safe workplace for its employees and others who are affected by the business. A company that fails to do this can be prosecuted (where they have five or more employees) for failing to comply with health and safety obligations. A company needs to appoint a health and safety champion, have a clear health and safety policy, and have minutes recording how it is going to deliver its policy. The directors need to ensure that all the company's decisions reflect its health and safety policy. The code also requires the company to consult its workforce on health and safety issues.

6

Keeping the statutory records

The duties of company secretaries include compliance with the legal requirement that private and public companies maintain statutory registers. Table 6.1 is a summary of the registers that should be kept.

Table 6.1   Company registers

Register	Description	Companies Act Reference
Members	Accounts detailing:	s352 CA1985
	– shareholder names	
	– addresses (if a confidentiality order is in place, use the service address)	
	– date of registration	
	– date of cessation of membership	
	– type, class and number of shares held	
	– amount paid	
	– the amount and class of stock held (if applicable)	
	– the class to which a member belongs (if the company does not have a share capital but does have different classes of member)	

Table 6.1   continued

Register	Description	Companies Act Reference
	Note. Where there is only one shareholder a statement to this effect must be added together with the date it became a single member company	
Directors and secretaries	*Directors:*	s288 CA1985 s289 CA1985 s290 CA1985
	Name or corporate name (and former name if appropriate), residential address and nationality, business occupation, details of other UK directorships, date of birth, former UK directorships held in the preceding five years. Dates of appointment and resignation to the offices stated	
	Secretaries:	
	Name or corporate company (and former name if appropriate), residential address (or service address, if a confidentiality order is in place) (registered or principal office address if a corporation). Dates of appointment and resignation to the offices are usually stated. If joint secretaries, then details of each secretary should be given	
	Note. When partners of a firm are joint secretaries give name of firm and principal office address	
Directors' interests	Name of director, information received, date of entry, date of grant, grants of rights to take up shares/debentures, duration, consideration of share(s), description and number of shares/debentures, price payable, that the right has been exercised and details thereof	s325 CA1985
Charges	Charges affecting company property/ floating charges on undertaking or property; description of property charged, amount of charge, persons entitled (except for securities to bearer), dates of the satisfaction of mortgages and charges	s407 CA1985 (s422 for Scottish companies)

Register	Description	Companies Act Reference
Minute book	Minutes of: – directors' (managers') meetings – general meetings – written resolutions – resolutions of the sole shareholder	s382 CA1985 s382(a) CA1985
Transfers	Date of transfer, name and address of transferor and transferee, log number of transfer, class and number of shares transferred, nominal value and consideration	Not statutory
Allotments	Date of allotment, log number, name and address of allottee, number of shares applied for and allotted, consideration, index number of shares	Not statutory
Seals	Date of sealing, log number, description of document sealed, date of authority by board, name(s) of officers using the seal	Not statutory
Debenture holders	Date of issue, name and address of holder, amount, release date (satisfaction), description	s190 CA1985
Substantial interests in shares (plcs only)	Name and address of person, information, date of notification to company index number, date of interest acquired date notifiable percentage attained, subsequent charges, and (for quoted companies) date and time of Stock Exchange announcement	s211 CA1985

The company secretary is responsible for the updating and keeping of the records. Whenever changes occur (for example, change of address for a director) the company secretary will need to ensure that the books are amended to reflect any change and Companies House advised (ie on *Form 288c*). The details of the company's shareholders need to be up to date so that any notices for general meetings and dividends are sent to the correct addresses.

The registers – electronic or manual

Companies are allowed to hold certain company registers on computer. This is increasingly popular with company secretaries burdened with the administration of a large number of companies or shareholders.

There are currently several company secretarial packages available to cater for the needs of the secretary. This software can store all the statutory and non-statutory registers and provide hardcopy printouts. A good package will include the facility to print Companies House forms, stock transfer forms, share certificates, dividend vouchers, etc. This can remove the need for the secretary to repeat the entry of the same name and address for shareholders and directors on several documents. The software publishers have to obtain the approval of Companies House for use of the printed forms.

Often a package will include a diary of events which can be used as a checklist for annual activities (such as filing accounts). This is particularly useful when the secretary is dealing with the administration of more than one company. One should also ask whether the package can file forms electronically at Companies House.

It is also important to remember that the storage of personal information (for example, names and addresses) is subject to the Data Protection Act 1998 and companies must be registered under the Act if this information is to be stored.

The computerization of records can allow directors to produce reports quickly for meetings and to keep track when patterns of unusual share transactions are taking place.

Manual records are, however, perfectly adequate to meet statutory requirements, especially where few changes are anticipated. A combined company register is usually supplied by company registration agents when a company is purchased off the shelf. These types of register are also available from law stationers.

It is important that the company's statutory books are completed and any changes entered as soon as is practicable after the event. When necessary, the company's accountants, as part of their audit, will review the statutory records. You should be aware that certain people have a right to view company registers (for example, shareholders have a right to inspect the register of members) and the register of directors and secretaries can be inspected by members of the public.

Security

It is important that the company's records and statutory books are securely stored. The company secretary should ensure that the records are kept in a locked cabinet or office free from damp and other environmental hazards. Companies House will keep an electronic record of forms filed with the Registrar. It is the responsibility of the company secretary to maintain a full set of records. It is recommended that the records in Figure 6.1 are kept permanently.

1. Certificate of Incorporation
2. A copy of the Memorandum and Articles of Association
3. Register of members
4. Register of directors and secretaries
5. Register of directors' interests
6. Register of charges
7. Minute books, including board and general meeting minutes
8. Letters to shareholders
9. Insurance policies
10. A copy of the directors' report and accounts for each year
11. Stock transfer forms
12. Cancelled share certificates

Figure 6.1   Suggested list of documents to be permanently stored

Where the company has a seal, steps should also be taken to ensure that this is kept securely in a safe or a locked cabinet. It is good company secretarial practice to ensure that each use of the seal is recorded with the appropriate entry in the register of seals. This can ensure that each document sealed is given a unique reference number.

Users of computerized records are advised to maintain daily backups, duplicate records and off-site storage of copies in the event of disaster. Security of systems is particularly important and it is usual for a series of passwords to be maintained to enable access to various levels of sensitive information. These passwords should be changed regularly, and should not be easy to guess or systematically discover. You should treat the access of computer information as if it were in the form of manual records that are stored safely.

A 'firewall' protecting the computer system from infiltration from outside, including the possibility of infection from computer viruses, should be maintained.

7

Annual routines

At the end of the accounting reference period the company secretary has a series of duties to perform. In particular, the secretary should be aware that the failure to file company accounts by the due date can lead to an automatic penalty, which for private limited companies is on a sliding scale from £100 to £1000. The maximum penalty for a plc is £5000! Details of late filing penalties can be found in *Late Filing Penalties – GBA5* available from Companies House.

There have been some recent changes following the introduction of SI2004 – The Companies Act 1985 (International Accounting Standards and Other Accounting Amendments) Regulations. This will impact on financial years that began on or after 1 January 2005. It gives all companies the opportunity to prepare their accounts under International Accounting Standards (IAS) rather than UK GAAP. For companies that continue to use UK GAAP there are changes to; how and where dividends are disclosed, how items must be presented in the balance sheet and the profit and loss account, and to the disclosure of information on derivatives. Key additional changes include:

■ abolishing the filing extension previously permitted to companies with overseas interests under Section 244;
■ changes for parent companies on the options and requirements on consolidation;

- directors' report to disclose financial instruments (not applicable to small companies);
- audit reports (new requirements).

Following the accounting scandals at Enron and Worldcom, the US Sarbanes–Oxley Act 2002 applies to companies that are required to file reports under the US Securities Exchange Act of 1934 or have filed registration statements under the US Securities Act 1933 (and have not withdrawn them). This affects all dual-listed companies and other non-US companies that make US-registered public offerings. The company secretary of a UK company needs to be aware of these US requirements as they may impact on companies incorporated outside the United States.

Accounts/financial statements

Every company must prepare accounts/financial statements and keep accounting records. A company's financial year is determined by its accounting reference date (ARD). A new company will have to prepare accounts from its date of incorporation to the ARD. After incorporation a company has nine months in which to give notice of its accounting reference date (see Chapter 4). A company's accounting reference period must not exceed 18 months; the date can be changed but notice must be given to Companies House (on the prescribed form).

The directors are responsible for the preparation of company accounts and for compliance with the requirements of the Companies Act 1985. Disclosure and filing exemptions are available for companies defined in the Act by their size as small or medium. A small company (non-group) must meet at least two of three following qualifications: an annual turnover of not more than £5.6 million; a balance sheet total of not more than £2.8 million; and average number of employees not more than 50. A company is defined as medium sized when it meets at least two of the following requirements: a turnover of not more than £22.8 million; a balance sheet total of not more than £11.4 million; or an average number of employees not more than 250. There are additional criteria and the website at Companies House should be consulted.

Accounts must be approved by the board of directors and be signed and dated on behalf of the board by a director. The director's signature must be on the company's balance sheet. Where a director's report is prepared, this must be approved by the board and be signed and dated on behalf of the board by a director or the company secretary. If auditors are required or appointed, a report signed and dated by the auditors must be included. Only original signatures will be accepted on accounts filed with the Registrar of Companies.

With effect from 1 January 2005 the right to claim a filing extension for companies with overseas business is being slowly removed. The regulation allowed companies to file for an extension for accounting periods that started before 1 January 2005. Companies that commenced their accounting periods on or after 1 January 2005 will have to make an application to the Secretary of State for a discretionary extension. This is really for more extreme situations where an event has occurred which was beyond the control of the board. Any application made under s244(5) will need to be in writing, giving reasons for the requirement of an extension and it must be filed before the expiration of the current accounting deadline.

A private limited company must file its accounts within the 10 months after the accounting reference date, with the following exception. New limited companies that have an accounting period in excess of 12 months from the date of incorporation have their filing period reduced to 22 months from incorporation. For plcs the period in such circumstances is 19 months. A public limited company has seven months within which to file accounts. One point to watch out for is that the end of the given period will end on the same date, in the appropriate month, as the ARD or, where there is no corresponding date, the last day of that month. This means that a company with an ARD of 30 September has until 30 July and **not** 31 July to file its accounts. The accounts do not have to be approved by the Inland Revenue before they are filed at Companies House.

Where a company has defective accounts that need a voluntary revision they are regulated by SI 2005/2282 and must be subject to the same process of approval as applied to the set of accounts being replaced. If there is a complete set of accounts replacing the ones filed, they must include a prominent statement to confirm that they replace the original for the financial period and that the revised accounts have been prepared at the same date as the original. As well as this, an explanation of non-compliance and details of any significant amendments must also be supplied.

Dormant companies

When the company has not traded during the financial year, it can be classed as dormant. The dormant company provisions *do not* apply to banking or insurance companies or to a person authorized under the Financial Services Act 1986. A company is defined as dormant in the Companies Act 1985 when it does not have any 'significant accounting transaction' in the relevant period. However, new companies are allowed to record the issue of subscriber shares within the period. Dormant companies will have to file dormant company accounts with the Registrar.

If a company becomes dormant, it can prepare dormant accounts in accordance with s249AA, provided it has been dormant since the end of the previous financial year, there was no requirement to prepare group accounts for that year and it qualifies as a small company under the Companies Act in relation to that year. Further information can be found in the Companies House booklet *GB10* or use the DCA format.

International Accounting Standards

Companies that have their financial year commencing on or after 1 January 2005 and whose shares are being traded as a regulated market (in the EU) will need to use the International Accounting Standards to prepare their accounts. In the UK the EU regulation allows its use by companies whose shares are traded publicly and non-traded companies (not charities) to use International Accounting Standards in their own or consolidated accounts.

Audit exempt companies

With effect from 11 August 1994, the requirement for an audit for certain small companies was abolished. Currently this applies where the company is small and the annual turnover is not more than £5.6 million and gross balance sheet assets are not more than £2.8 million. For a charity to qualify as small, its gross income is more than £90,000 but not more than £250,000 and its balance sheet for the year is not more than £1.4 million.

Certain companies are excluded from using these exemptions, for example where the company was public in any part of the year, or was either a parent or a subsidiary, or a bank, insurance company or regulated by the Financial Services and Markets Act 2000. However, the Companies Act (Operating and Financial Review and Directors Reports etc) Regulation 2005 (SI 2005/1001) has amended the act so that small financial services companies carrying out mortgage advisory work or insurance mediation may be exempt from audit where they are also within the small company definition. This exclusion from the exemption also applies if the company was a member of a group at any time in the year, although where the group qualifies as a small group, it may still be possible to be exempt from an audit.

An audit exempt company will still need to file accounts at Companies House and have a statement on the balance sheet saying that it was eligible to take advantage of the exemption. Full unaudited accounts will still need to be presented to the members of the company. Companies House is aiming to introduce e-filing to non-audited accounts.

It is worth noting that the Companies (Defective Accounts) (Authorised Persons) Order 2005 is law. It permits the Financial Reporting Review Panel to make an application for a court order for the directors to prepare revised accounts when the annual accounts do not comply with the Companies Act 1985.

Operating and Financial Reviews were introduced as a reporting requirement for quoted companies under the Draft Companies Act 1985 (Operating and Financial Review and Directors Report) Regulations 2005, but this has now been abolished by the government; however the OFR is best practice. The main issue is that public companies will still have to comply with the EU directives which require similar disclosures.

Annual general meeting

Every company must hold an annual general meeting within 18 months of the date of incorporation. Thereafter, annual general meetings must be held each year and no more than 15 months apart. The annual general meeting is usually held each year and where the directors present the shareholders with the company's accounts for adoption. Other formal ordinary business usually dealt with includes the declaration of a dividend (if one is to be paid), the retirement and re-election of directors (if necessary) and the (re)appointment of auditors as appropriate and to approve their remuneration (or to authorize the directors to approve fees). The ICSA recommends that special business to be conducted should be accompanied by an explanation. It is a requirement that the full text of a special resolution is given in the notice of the AGM. The notice must also state when a resolution is to be proposed as a special resolution.

It is the responsibility of the company secretary to prepare and send out notices of the annual general meeting when instructed to by the board. Table A of the Companies (Tables A–F) Regulations 1985 requires that the notice state the general nature of the business of the meeting to be transacted. The company secretary should check the Articles of Association for procedure and type of business to be conducted. Each resolution should be stated separately so that the shareholders can vote on each individual proposal.

The meeting gives the directors an opportunity to report on the profitability or otherwise of the company and also gives shareholders the chance to question the directors about the company and their conduct of its affairs. The company secretary will need to ensure that the meeting runs smoothly by providing the chairman with a detailed agenda and briefing him or her before the meeting. For public companies, such an event may have media interest and smooth running is therefore vital.

Shareholders of a private limited company must be given at least 21 clear days' notice of an annual general meeting. Good practice dictates that 20 working days' notice of the AGM should be given if possible. It can be held on shorter notice, however, if this is agreed by all the members entitled to attend and vote at the meeting.

Under the Directors' Remuneration Report Regulations 2002, quoted companies must publish a report on directors' remuneration as approved by the board, and put a resolution to shareholders on the report at each AGM. The Association of British Insurers (ABI) published its own guidelines on executive pay in December 2002. It requires boards to consult with investors when deciding on their remuneration policy, and to show that performance-based pay is aligned with the company's strategy.

The Company Reform White Paper (March 2005) will make decision making easier for private limited companies, allowing them to make more decisions by written resolution. They can be carried by a 75 per cent majority rather than being made by unanimous consent, as it is at present.

Failure to hold an annual general meeting

When a company has failed to hold an annual general meeting, a shareholder can apply to the Secretary of State to call or direct the calling of a meeting. The Secretary of State can order the convening of an annual general meeting and give such other consequential directions as he or she considers expedient. Where default arises, the company and every officer is liable to a fine.

Dispensing with annual general meetings

Private companies can resolve (by elective resolution) to dispense with the holding of annual general meetings. Elective resolutions can also remove the obligation to present accounts and reports to a general meeting and the re-election of auditors (if necessary). The elective resolutions removing the obligation to present accounts has effect in relation to the financial year if it is passed and cannot remove an obligation relating to previous years. For example, one cannot elect to dispense with the laying of accounts for the year ended 30 June 2003 if it is now August 2003. In order for elective resolutions passed in general meeting to be effective they have to meet two criteria:

1. Twenty-one clear days' notice in writing is given of the meeting stating that an elective resolution is to be proposed and setting out full details of the resolution.

2. The resolution must be agreed by *all members* entitled to vote at the meeting.

A signed copy of the elective resolution must be filed at Companies House within 15 days of its being passed. If you are considering passing an elective resolution, you should check the company's Articles of Association to ensure that there are no conflicting rules concerning annual general meetings. Elective resolutions can also be passed by written resolution(s) of all the members.

When elective resolutions have been passed, which include the dispensation to present accounts, a shareholder has the right to request a general meeting be held for this purpose. The Companies Act requires that copies of the final accounts be sent out to the shareholders at least 28 days before the end of the period allowed for presenting accounts, together with a letter to each shareholder advising of their right to require the laying of accounts and reports before a general meeting. Any shareholder or auditor who requires a general meeting to be held must send a notice to the company's registered office within 28 days of the accounts being posted. If the directors fail to respond to this request within 21 days, the general meeting can be called by the person who sent the notice.

There is a proposal in the new Companies Bill that suggests that public companies might be allowed, upon a unanimous vote, to dispense with Annual General Meetings and the presentation of accounts. The new bill also proposes that private companies will no longer have to hold AGMs or present accounts unless they adopt what is called a 'Mandatory Regime'. All companies formed under the new Companies Act will be automatically exempted from holding AGMs. Companies formed under previous legislation will opt out by using a special resolution. A company can return to the mandatory regime by an ordinary resolution.

Annual return forms

Form 363a, the annual return form, must be filed by every registered company.

This form is a summary of required statutory information about the company. By keeping the company's registers up to date, the secretary will find the return easy to complete. The annual return form is reproduced in Appendix 1 (see pages 112–51).

E-copies of annual returns can be filed by using company secretarial software packages that are available. Companies House now provides a Web Filing service on its website. The fee for e-returns is £15 as opposed to written returns which cost £30. A useful list of providers of electronic filing can be found on the Companies House website www.companieshouse.gov.uk/toolstohelp/efsoftwaresupp.shtml.

Form 363s is partially completed by Companies House and is referred to as a shuttle return. Do not presume that the information supplied on this form is correct. It will have to be checked and amended where necessary. Other details may have to be added manually, including business activities, the location of the register of members and debenture holders. Once you have entered the business activities in the first annual return, this is a completed section on the shuttle annual return. Companies House, sends out annual returns with the information about share capital and shareholders pre-printed in the shuttle forms (where there are under 20 members). Where the annual return is the first one prepared after incorporation, a schedule of past and present shareholders and their holdings will have to be included. Details of shareholders must be supplied at least every three years thereafter if there have been no changes in the period. If, however, there have been share transactions during the year, a schedule of past and present members must be filed with the appropriate return. The completed form must be signed and dated by a director or secretary of the company.

If you have not received a partially completed *Form 363s*, you can either telephone the appropriate section at Companies House and ask for a duplicate or obtain *Form 363a* from Companies House stationery office, where it is available free of charge.

The company is obliged to file an annual return form each year made up to a date not later than the anniversary of the company's incorporation. The date to which the annual return is made up is called the **legal return date**. Annual returns must be filed within 28 days of the legal return date. The signed annual return, together with the appropriate fee, must be filed at Companies House. Failure to file a return within the 28 days will result in an offence and the company and officers being liable to a fine. In the case of continued default a daily fine may be payable.

It is possible to alter the legal return date. However, Companies House will not accept a return made up to the new date if both it and the previous return were filed late.

8

Extraordinary events

The company will, from time to time, need to make various statutory changes and this chapter gives a selection of events that may arise. You should treat this information as introductory and refer to other sources of advice for reference where complex changes are to be tackled.

Resolutions

When a meeting considers an act or event to be carried out, the business considered is referred to as a **motion**. Once the motion has been expressed, the meeting will consider its terms. When approved, the motion is transformed into a **resolution**. A resolution as finally agreed may, of course, be different from the original as it is possible that amendments are made during the debate but the difference cannot be material. You should be aware that although the Companies Act refers to motions and resolutions synonymously, the separate definitions given above should be applied in this chapter.

The Companies Act 1985 provides for the following main types of resolution:

- ordinary resolutions;
- elective resolutions;

▓ extraordinary resolutions;
▓ special resolutions.

In addition, reference is made to resolutions by motion type, ie directors' resolutions, class resolutions, and written resolutions. Resolutions can be defined by meeting type or the method by which they are passed. For example, class resolutions are passed by a particular class of shareholders. Written resolutions can, where authorized by the Articles of Association or under the Act for private companies, be passed by directors and shareholders. There is a special procedure for members' written resolutions.

Written resolutions are referred to in Table A of the Companies (Tables A to F) Regulations 1985 which permits a resolution in writing signed by all the members entitled to receive notice and attend general meetings to be as valid and effective as if it has been passed at a general meeting. This clause in Table A may be included in the Articles of Association. Private companies can use the statutory procedure for written resolutions under s381A when the provision in Table A has not been adopted. Under the Act a written resolution does not have effect unless a copy is given to the company's auditors at or before the time the resolution is supplied to the member(s) for signature.

The procedure under the Act for written resolutions cannot be used to remove a director or an auditor before expiration of their terms of office (ss303 and 391 Companies Act 1985). There are also additional requirements for statutory written resolutions in certain circumstances, for example: where pre-emption rights on allotment are waived; financial assistance is given for the purchase of the company's own shares or those of the holding company; authority is given for an off-market purchase or a contingent purchase of the company's own shares; approval for payment out of capital; the funding of a director's expenditure in performing his or her duties; and the approval of a director's service contract.

Ordinary resolutions

These resolutions require only a simple majority (greater than 50 per cent) of those entitled to vote at a meeting. They are the most frequently used type of resolution for business matters at board and general meetings. In general meetings, ordinary resolutions will normally be used for routine business matters, for example to increase the company's share capital, to approve directors' service contracts, to renew the directors' authority to allot shares or securities, to capitalise profits, to reappoint the auditor, and to declare dividends.

In general, it is not necessary for ordinary resolutions to be set out verbatim in the notice of the meeting; it is quite common, however, for them to be set out in full. Ordinary resolutions do not as a rule need to be notified to Companies House. There are, however, exceptions which must by law be notified, for example increases in share capital and renewal of the directors' authority to allot securities. The Companies Act specifies those resolutions of the board which must be filed at Companies House.

Elective resolutions

These types of resolution can only be passed by a private company. All the shareholders must agree at a general meeting, or in writing, to the passing of an elective resolution. A minimum of 21 days' notice in writing of the general meeting must be given to all shareholders of the terms of the proposed resolution for it to be valid. Elective resolutions were introduced by the Companies Act 1989 in order to permit deregulation of statutory obligations in the following circumstances:

1. to dispense with the obligation to hold annual general meetings;
2. to dispense with the requirement to present a directors' report and accounts to the shareholders at general meetings;
3. to dispense with the requirement to (re)appoint auditors annually;
4. to permit the directors' authority to issue shares or securities to continue for a fixed or indefinite period;
5. to allow the proportion of members required to consent to the calling of an extraordinary general meeting at short notice to be reduced from 95 per cent to a minimum of 90 per cent of all eligible shareholders.

An elective resolution can be revoked by an ordinary resolution and will also cease to be effective if the company is re-registered as a public company. Although an elective resolution will be effective even if there are contrary terms in the Articles of Association, it is advisable to amend the Articles accordingly. A signed copy of an elective resolution must be filed at Companies House within 15 days of being passed. An ordinary resolution revoking the elective resolution must also be filed within 15 days of being passed.

Extraordinary resolutions

An extraordinary resolution requires a 75 per cent majority of shareholders voting in person, or by proxy, at a general meeting. The amount of notice to be given of the meeting depends on the type of meeting at which it is to be proposed. A resolution to be proposed at an extraordinary general meeting requires 14 clear days' notice and an annual general meeting needs 21 clear days. Extraordinary resolutions can be used, for example, to vary the class rights of shareholders. A signed copy of an extraordinary resolution must be filed at Companies House within 15 days of being passed.

Special resolutions

These also require a 75 per cent majority of members in general meeting for them to be passed but at least 21 clear days' notice of the general meeting at which the resolution is to be passed must be given. The definition of 'clear days' may be found in Table A, but this may be modified by the Articles of Association. Shorter notice, however, may be given if so agreed by those shareholders entitled to attend and vote at the meeting (90 per cent when elective resolution variation or 95 per cent agreement for an extraordinary general meeting and 100 per cent for an annual general meeting). By law, a special resolution is required by each of the following:

1. to amend the Articles of Association;
2. to change the objects clause of the Memorandum of Association;
3. to change the company name;
4. to reduce the company's share capital;
5. to allow a private company to give financial assistance for the purchase of its own shares;
6. to resolve that the company be dormant;

7. to re-register a private limited company as a public limited company;
8. to re-register an unlimited company as a private limited company;
9. to re-register a public limited company as a private limited company;
10. to remove pre-emption rights on the allotment of shares.

Amendments to resolutions

An ordinary resolution (if set out in full in the notice of the meeting) may be amended within the scope of the notice and passed with amendments at the meeting at which it is considered. The notices of the meetings at which it is intended to move a special or an extraordinary resolution must contain the entire substance of the resolution. Extraordinary and special resolutions cannot therefore be varied or amended at the meeting. If a relevant amendment to an extraordinary or special resolution can be made, it must be set before another meeting of which the requisite notice has been given (of course, minor spelling or grammatical errors may be corrected if the alterations are not substantive). It is fundamental that the amendment is one that does not involve any departure from the substance of the resolution as in the original notice of the meeting.

Companies House publishes a booklet entitled *Resolutions – GBA7* which summarizes the requirements.

Board changes

The following sections concern the necessary actions for changes of directors. In the case of a change of company secretary, the procedure is different as they are appointees of the board. You should refer to the checklists given in Chapter 4 for the correct procedure.

Appointments and resignations

The procedure to appoint or approve the resignation of a director has been outlined in Chapter 4. You can use the same checklists, draft letters and minutes shown for the appointment/resignation of directors.

Cessations and removals

A cessation occurs when a director ceases to act in accordance with the company's Articles of Association and other than by resignation (for example, removal or death). The company secretary will need to ensure that this is recorded in the minutes of the next board meeting and that notice is given to Companies House (*Form 288b* – see page 131). The appropriate entries must be made in the registers of directors and directors' interests.

A company may, by ordinary resolution, remove a director under the provisions of the Companies Act 1985 (s303). This can be done before the end of the director's term of office and regardless of any provisions in the Articles of Association or any agreement it may have with him or her. Special notice of 28 days is required for this resolution. You should be aware that removal will not necessarily deprive a director of the right to compensation or damages arising from the termination of his or her appointment as director. Additionally, the Articles may contain alternative provisions (see Chapter 5).

A director has a right to protest to a resolution proposed for his or her removal. A director is entitled to be heard at the meeting at which the resolution is to be proposed and to submit written representations for circulation to the shareholders (if not received too late). If these representations are received too late or the company is in default in not sending them to members, the director may require that the representations be read out at the general meeting. These responses will not need to be read out if a successful application has been made to the court by the company or any other party claiming to be aggrieved. It would be advisable to obtain the appropriate legal advice before proceeding with this course of action.

The Articles usually contain provisions for a director to vacate his or her office on the occurrence of various offences, for example disqualification or becoming of unsound mind (see Chapter 4 for a comprehensive list).

Share transactions

A discussion in Chapter 5 covers part of the procedure for the non-market transfers of shares. There are circumstances where the change in ownership of shares may occur other than by a normal transfer, for example death, insanity, liquidation of corporate shareholder, or bankruptcy. This type of change of ownership is referred to as the **transmission of shares**.

Transmission of shares

The formal requirements for the transfer of shares do not apply in all cases. Transmission by operation of law, on the death of a shareholder for example, means that the legal title of his or her shares passes automatically to that shareholder's legal representatives (or, if the shares were held in joint names, to the surviving shareholder). Company secretaries in England and Wales will deal with a different procedure to those in Scotland when dealing with grants of probate or letters of administration. The procedure is complicated and depends upon various factors, such as whether or not a will was made. A flow diagram (see Figure 8.1), intended as a guide for the various situations that may arise, is given. Registration in the names of personal representatives, trustees in bankruptcy or a receiver is instigated by letter of request. There is no prescribed form for the letter of request unless the Articles so provide. A company must accept the production to it of the grant of probate or letters of administration as sufficient evidence of the grant.

It is possible that the shares may need to be left registered in the name of the deceased person until the administration is complete. Shares are transferable by the personal representatives whether or not they have been registered as members in their own right. You should ensure that the executor's name and address are entered on the register of members for notices and dividends. A letter of request is normally completed by the executor and forwarded to the company secretary to ask for their name to be put on the register of members.

Change of shareholder name/address

Shareholders may wish to change their name (for example, on marriage or divorce) or address and you will be asked to amend the register of members. Documentary evidence should be provided to show the name change and, when satisfied, the register of members can be amended.

The date of the change of name should be inserted. The previous entry should be neatly crossed out with a single line, but still be readable, as it forms part of the company records.

A marriage certificate is sufficient evidence of a change of name, as is a deed poll. A copy should be kept with the register for future reference.

Joint shareholders

Shares can be registered in the names of two or more people or companies. The shares will be acquired in joint names but only one address will be recorded – the address of the first named shareholder. Correspondence such as notices of general meetings and other letters to shareholders will be sent to this address. The Articles of Association will provide the procedure with regard to the voting rights of joint shareholders. Normally these are exercised by the first named holder. You should check the Articles for restrictions on the numbers of joint shareholders when there are more than two names (for example, some Articles restrict the maximum number of names to four).

Dividends

If a company has traded profitably it may wish to distribute part of its net profit to its shareholders in proportion to their shareholding. Payment of dividends is governed by the Memorandum and Articles of the paying company which must always be examined for any special provisions. Whether or not a company is able to declare a dividend by making a distribution of net profits (or assets) will be determined by reference to the restrictions in the Companies Act 1985. Private and public companies can only declare dividends out of profits available for distribution. These are its accumulated, realized profits so far as not previously distributed or capitalised, less its accumulated, realized losses so far as not previously written off in a reduction or a reorganisation of capital. You should consult the company's accountant to ensure that a distribution can be made, if you are unsure about it.

Dividends declared may be either **interim** or **final**. Interim dividends subject to the Memorandum and Articles can be declared by directors during the financial year if there are sufficient profits. If the

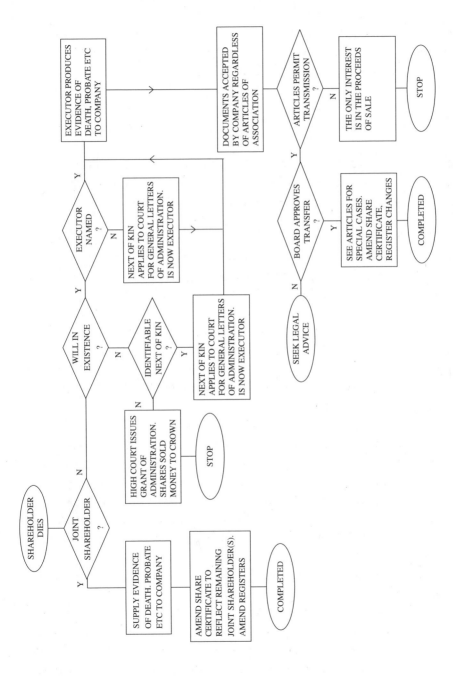

Figure 8.1 Flow diagram summarizing procedure of transmission of shares following the death of a shareholder

directors wish to declare a final dividend, they must obtain, at the annual general meeting, the approval of the members who may not increase the amount above that recommended. Payment of a dividend may be approved by ordinary resolution. Prior to the declaration of a dividend, you will need to check the company's Articles of Association for the dividend rights attaching to different classes of shares.

You should ensure that any decision to pay, or recommend, a dividend is recorded in the board and general meeting minutes. It is normal that the resolution records the date on which the dividend is declared, and that it will apply only to those names in the register of members on the date specified in the resolution. Some companies close their register of members for a period of up to a maximum 30 days in order to prepare lists for dividend payments. Following the declaration of a dividend, the secretary through delegated or authorized authority should prepare cheques in the amounts due to each shareholder. These are sent out with a covering letter, which is referred to as a **dividend voucher**, which needs to be returned by the shareholder.

Registration of mortgages and charges

As discussed in Chapter 6, a register of charges must be kept. Legal charges secure borrowing of the company by way of, for example, a mortgage or a fixed, or floating, charge. **Fixed charges** are created on a particular asset (for example, the leasehold or freehold of a property). **Floating charges** constitute a general charge on all the assets of a company. A floating charge fastens upon and specifically binds the charged assets which are in existence when some event occurs which crystallizes the charge.

When the company borrows money from a bank, or other lending organization, the lender will invariably require a charge as security for the loan. The lender will usually file notification of any charge created at Companies House, although it is the company's duty to register the charge. Notification of charges must be filed within 21 days of their creation. Details of this charge will need to be entered in your register of charges. When the loan has been repaid (the charge is satisfied), notification must be filed at Companies House of this event. A declaration of satisfaction and release (*Forms 403a* and *403b* – see pages 146 and 147) is sworn by an officer of the company before a solicitor or commissioner of oaths and filed at Companies House.

Details of the satisfaction of a charge need to be entered in the register of charges.

Resolving to change the company name

If you wish to change the company name, first you will need to check whether the proposed name is available (see general discussion of choosing names in Chapter 3). The procedure is outlined in Table 8.1.

Initially, the directors will need to approve a resolution to change the company name. A special resolution of shareholders must then be passed – at an extraordinary general meeting, at an annual general meeting, or by written resolution, whichever is the most convenient (and permissible under the Articles of Association).

After the special resolution has been filed at Companies House (within 15 days of being passed) together with the fee, the Registrar will issue a Certificate of Incorporation on Change of Name. This usually takes about a week. An application for a change of name can be made on a same-day basis. For this service a premium fee of £50 is payable. If you need to effect a name change on a particular date, you should contact Companies House well in advance (at least 14 days) of the date required and file the resolution together with a letter requesting that the change of name take place on the particular date. An example of a resolution to change a company name is given in Figure 8.2.

Changing Memorandum and Articles of Association

A company may wish to alter its Articles of Association (and, less frequently, its Memorandum of Association).

Table 8.1   Checklist of procedure on change of company name

Action	✓
1. Check name availability and whether special permission is required to use certain words in the name (see Chapter 3)	
2. Hold a board meeting to: – pass resolution to change the name – authorize secretary to convene EGM (alternatively use AGM or written resolution)	
3. Send out notice of meeting (**NB.** Notice required for EGM is 21 clear days for a special resolution); alternatively circulate a written resolution to the members	
4. Hold meeting, special resolution passed by more than 75 per cent majority	
5. File signed resolution at Companies House (see example below) with fee of £20 (or £50 if a same-day change is required)	
After receipt of incorporation certificate on change of name	
6. Affix a copy of the resolution to the front of all copies of the Memorandum and Articles of Association and (if practicable) reprint in the new name	
7. Amend company documentation (eg headed notepaper, invoices, etc)	
8. Notify advisors/others (accountants, solicitors, banks, etc)	
9. Order new nameplate (and seal if necessary)	

Alteration of the Memorandum of Association is possible, but less likely, due to the increasing use of general commercial company objects. Where a company wishes to alter, expand or limit its objects, a checklist for the procedure is given in Table 8.2.

Subject to the provisions of the Companies Act 1985 and to the conditions contained in its Memorandum, a company may, by special resolution, alter its Articles. A change to the company's Articles of Association can be carried out by using the same general checklist as for amending the Memorandum of Association using steps 1 to 4 and 6. There is no automatic right of objection to an alteration. Any special

Company Number: 145567

THE COMPANIES ACT 1985

COMPANY LIMITED BY SHARES

SPECIAL RESOLUTION

of

DASHWOOD & SONS LIMITED

Passed on   2003

At an Extraordinary General Meeting of the Company duly held at Felix House, Dogget Road, Chatham, Kent on the   day of   2003 the following resolution was duly passed:

THAT the company name be changed to:

DASHWOOD & SONS (UK) LIMITED

CHAIRMAN/DIRECTOR

DATED:

Figure 8.2   Change of company name resolution

Table 8.2   Checklist of procedure on change of Memorandum of Association

Action	✓

1. Hold a board meeting to:
  – resolve to amend the objects and approve wording of resolution to be put to the members
  – authorize secretary to convene EGM (alternatively, use AGM or written resolution)
  – if necessary, prepare and circulate letter to shareholders explaining reasons for change	

2. Send out notice of meeting:
  – include letter from chairman explaining reasons for change
  – information copies to preference share/debenture holders (for those who do not have a vote)
  – special resolution, 21 days' notice	

3. Hold meeting, special resolution passed by more than 75 per cent majority	
4. File signed resolution at Companies House	

5. Objections can be made by share or debenture holders (15 per cent or more) up to 21 days after the meeting:
 	
  – if application has been made to court for cancellation of the alteration of Memorandum then notice of application must be filed at Companies House (Form 6)
  – if application is successful, court may impose a compromise	

6. If application is unsuccessful or no application has been made, amend printed copy of Memorandum (and Articles) of Association and file at Companies House within 15 days	

resolution passed takes effect immediately. You should ensure that any professional advisors (for example accountants) are notified of any change.

Changing auditors

Dormant and audit exempt companies do not need to appoint auditors, therefore the following details will not apply to these types of company.

Where auditors have to be appointed, a private company may choose to pass an elective resolution to dispense with annual appointment (see Chapter 7). When this election is in force any shareholder may send a notice to the company's registered office proposing that the auditors' appointment be terminated. If this happens, it is the duty of the directors to convene a general meeting within 28 days of the notice, to propose a resolution in a form enabling the company to decide whether the appointment of the auditors should be brought to an end.

Where an election is not in force (see Chapter 4) the auditors will normally be reappointed at the annual general meeting.

Change will arise due to the removal, or resignation, of an auditor. A removal can be effected by an ordinary resolution at any time notwithstanding any agreement between the auditors and the company. Written resolutions cannot be used for this purpose. Special notice must be given of any resolution for the removal of an auditor and must be sent to the auditors who are entitled to make a written response to the company and request a copy of it to be sent to shareholders. The auditor who is to be removed is entitled to attend the meeting to address members on the subject of his or her removal. In certain circumstances, the auditor may require a written representation to be read out. A removed auditor may attend the meeting at which it is intended to fill the casual vacancy, and any meeting at which his or her term of office would have expired (ie the annual general meeting).

A *Form 391* (see page 145) must be filed within 14 days at Companies House to give notice of the removal of auditors.

Notice of the resignation of an auditor must be sent to the registered office of the company. The notice is not effective unless accompanied by the statement required by s394 of the Companies Act 1985. A copy of the auditor's resignation letter must be sent by the company secretary to the Registrar within 14 days of its receipt at the registered office. Resigning auditors have various rights and may choose to:

1. give, in the notice, a statement of circumstances which exist that they consider should be brought to the attention of shareholders and/or creditors;
2. exercise the right to requisition the calling of an extraordinary general meeting, to receive an explanation of the reasons for resigning;

3. require the company to circulate a statement containing reasons for resignation;
4. request that the notice of the general meeting refers to the statement made in (3) above.

When a company changes its auditors between annual general meetings, this creates a casual vacancy. The directors can appoint an auditor to fill a casual vacancy between annual general meetings. Where this has occurred, special notice (28 days) must be given of their reappointment at the next general meeting. The removal process in practice does not need to be used very often as auditors will usually resign upon request.

9

Dissolution

There are occasions when a company may no longer be required such as after the sale of the business or on insolvency. When your company is no longer required you will need to arrange for it to be dissolved. The existence of a company may be brought to an end either by dissolution: either as the ultimate stage of a member's or creditor's voluntary winding up or a company's compulsory winding up; or as a result of the company's name being struck off by the Registrar; or by the court.

There are strict procedures set down in the Insolvency Act 1986 which must be followed for all voluntary (members' or creditors') winding up, and for winding up by the court. This procedure is complex and assistance will be needed from an insolvency practitioner. Introductory information concerning compulsory and voluntary liquidation is available from Companies House in *Liquidation and Insolvency – GBW1* and *Liquidation and Insolvency (Scotland) – GBW1(S)*.

Dissolution of a dormant company

Under s652A there is a procedure that is an inexpensive alternative to voluntary winding up for non-trading unwanted companies. If you wish to pursue this course of action, clearance should first be sought from the Inland Revenue.

Before you consider following this procedure, it is *essential* that you ensure that the company has no assets as on dissolution they will pass to the Crown as *bona vacantia*.

The striking off procedure

A company can apply for striking off unwanted private companies if, in the prior three months, it has not:

1. traded or carried on business in any way;
2. disposed of property or rights for value that were held immediately before ceasing to trade for disposal or gain;
3. changed the company name;
4. undertaken *any activity* other than applying for dissolution (the implication is that the company must have been dormant for at least three months).

Where the company is part of a group of companies, you need to check with the the in-house tax department or its advisors. In addition, you will also need approval from the Inland Revenue before the company can be struck-off. It is vital that you double check the company has no assets or liabilities. Some assets, such as licenses or intellectual property, may need to be transferred.

Any company that is the subject of insolvency proceedings or a compromise or an agreement is ineligible to use the s652 striking-off process. It is an offence to apply for a striking-off application if the company is ineligible.

A board meeting will need to be held where the directors note that the company is eligible to apply for striking off and to call for an extraordinary general meeting or to authorize the circulation of a written resolution for the members to approve the application. It is important to ensure that the company has no assets and has closed its bank account before embarking on this procedure. If a company is struck off and has a bank account its assets will be frozen.

It is vital that a company which is struck off under this procedure has no assets at the time it is struck off. Once a company is struck off (and it is registered in England and Wales) then its assets will belong to the crown (or the Duchy of Cornwall or Lancaster) and become *Bona vacantia* (5654), depending on the address of the registered office. If a company is accidentally struck off and holds assets, such as property or a bank account with cash in it, then the only remedy is to apply to court for the company to be restored to the register. An application for restoration is quite expensive. The risk with striking off of a private company is that it may be returned to the register within 20 years of the striking-off application.

After the meetings have been held a *Form 652a* (and *Form 652a (cont)* if necessary) must either be signed by the sole director or be signed by a majority of the directors, if there is more than one. *Form 652a* needs to be filed at Companies House for a fee of £10. Copies of *Form 652a* need to be sent by recorded delivery to any current (or new in the next seven days) shareholders, creditors, employees, managers or trustees of any pension fund, and the directors who have signed it.

Once the *Form 652a* has been filed at Companies House and accepted as a public record of the company, a letter is sent from Companies House to the applicant to confirm safe receipt. A notice will be published in the *Gazette* and after at least three months from the date of publication of the notice the company can be struck off by the Registrar.

If the company wishes to withdraw its application, it will need to fill in *Form 652c*. This application must be withdrawn if the company:

1. trades;
2. disposes of property rights of value;
3. changes its name;
4. undertakes any activity other than applying for dissolution.

Applicants must give copies of their request to persons connected with the company, ie directors, creditors, employees, shareholders, and the manager of the company's pension fund.

Striking off by the Registrar

The Registrar of Companies is empowered under s652 to strike a company off the register if he has reasonable cause to believe that the company is not carrying on business or in operation. This usually occurs if the company has failed to file its accounts and annual returns on time. Thus a company that is actually active can involuntarily be struck off if it fails to meet its filing obligations. As mentioned earlier, the assets will pass to the Crown or other bodies, and a court order will be required to recover those assets.

Appendix 1:

Copies of Companies House forms referred to in the text

Companies House Form Number	Title of Form	Chapter(s)
6	Cancellation of alteration to objects of a company	8
10	First directors and secretary and intended situation of registered office	3, 4
12	Declaration or application for registration	3, 4
88(2)	Return of allotments of shares	3, 5
88(3)	Particulars of a contract relating to shares allotted as fully or partly paid up otherwise than in cash	3, 5
190	Location of register of debenture holders	4
190a	Notice of place for inspection of a register of holders of debentures, which is kept in non-legible form, or of any change in that place	4

Companies House *Form* Number	Title of *Form*	Chapter(s)
225	Change of accounting reference date	3, 4
287	Change in situation or address of registered office	3, 4, 5
288a	Appointment of director or secretary	3, 4, 5
288b	Terminating appointment as director or secretary	3, 4, 5, 8
288c	Change of particulars for director or secretary	3, 4, 5, 6
318	Location of directors' service contracts	4
325	Location of the register of directors' interests in shares, etc	4
325a	Notice of place for inspection of a register of directors' interest in shares, etc, which is kept in non-legible form, or any change in that place	4
353	Register of members	4
353a	Notice of place for inspection of a register of members which is kept in a non-legible form, or of any change in that place	4
363a	Annual return	7
363a(sch) 363a(cont)	List of past and present members	7
363a	Annual return (*referred to as a shuttle return*)	7

Companies House Form Number	Title of *Form*	Chapter(s)
391	Notice of passing of resolution removing an auditor	8
403a	Declaration of satisfaction in full or in part of mortgage or charge	8
403b	Declaration that part of the property or undertaking (a) has been released from the charge; (b) no longer forms part of the company's property or undertaking	8
652a	Application for striking off	9
652a(cont)	Application for striking off (continuation sheet)	9
652c	Withdrawal of application for striking off	9

Companies House
—— *for the record* ——

Please complete in typescript,
or in bold black capitals.

CHFP000

6

Cancellation of alteration to the objects of a company

Company Number

Company Name in full

An application was made to the Court on:

Day Month Year

for the cancellation of the alteration made to the objects of the company by a special resolution passed on:

Day Month Year

Signed **Date**

† Please delete as appropriate.

† a director / secretary / administrator / administrative receiver / receiver manager / receiver

Please give the name, address, telephone number and, if available, a DX number and Exchange of the person Companies House should contact if there is any query.

Tel

DX number   DX exchange

Companies House receipt date barcode

This form has been provided free of charge by Companies House.

Form revised July 1998

When you have completed and signed the form please send it to the Registrar of Companies at:
Companies House, Crown Way, Cardiff, CF14 3UZ   DX 33050 Cardiff
for companies registered in England and Wales
or
Companies House, 37 Castle Terrace, Edinburgh, EH1 2EB
for companies registered in Scotland   **DX 235 Edinburgh**

Companies House
—— *for the record* ——

*Please complete in typescript,
or in bold black capitals.*
CHWP000

Notes on completion appear on final page

10

First directors and secretary and intended situation of registered office

Company Name in full

Proposed Registered Office

(PO Box numbers only, are not acceptable)

Post town

County / Region   Postcode

If the memorandum is delivered by an agent for the subscriber(s) of the memorandum mark the box opposite and give the agent's name and address.

Agent's Name

Address

Post town

County / Region   Postcode

Number of continuation sheets attached

You do not have to give any contact information in the box opposite but if you do, it will help Companies House to contact you if there is a query on the form. The contact information that you give will be visible to searchers of the public record.

Tel

DX number   DX exchange

Companies House receipt date barcode

This form has been provided free of charge by Companies House

v 10/03

When you have completed and signed the form please send it to the Registrar of Companies at:
Companies House, Crown Way, Cardiff, CF14 3UZ   DX 33050 Cardiff
for companies registered in England and Wales
or
Companies House, 37 Castle Terrace, Edinburgh, EH1 2EB
for companies registered in Scotland   DX 235 Edinburgh
                                                        or LP - 4 Edinburgh 2

Company Secretary (see notes 1-5)

Company name	
NAME *Style / Title	*Honours etc
* Voluntary details Forename(s)	
Surname	
Previous forename(s)	
Previous surname(s)	
Address ††	
Post town	
County / Region	Postcode
Country	

†† Tick this box if the address shown is a service address for the beneficiary of a Confidentiality Order granted under section 723B of the Companies Act 1985 otherwise, give your usual residential address. In the case of a corporation or Scottish firm, give the registered or principal office address.

I consent to act as secretary of the company named on page 1

Consent signature | **Date**

Directors (see notes 1-5)

Please list directors in alphabetical order

NAME *Style / Title	*Honours etc
Forename(s)	
Surname	
Previous forename(s)	
Previous surname(s)	
Address ††	
Post town	
County / Region	Postcode
Country	

†† Tick this box if the address shown is a service address for the beneficiary of a Confidentiality Order granted under section 723B of the Companies Act 1985 otherwise, give your usual residential address. In the case of a corporation or Scottish firm, give the registered or principal office address.

Date of birth Day Month Year | **Nationality**

Business occupation

Other directorships

I consent to act as director of the company named on page 1

Consent signature | **Date**

Directors (see notes 1-5)

Please list directors in alphabetical order

NAME *Style / Title		*Honours etc

* Voluntary details

Forename(s)

Surname

Previous forename(s)

Previous surname(s)

†† Tick this box if the address shown is a service address for the beneficiary of a Confidentiality Order granted under section 723B of the Companies Act 1985 otherwise, give your usual residential address. In the case of a corporation or Scottish firm, give the registered or principal office address.

Address ††

Post town

County / Region   **Postcode**

Country

Day   Month   Year

Date of birth   **Nationality**

Business occupation

Other directorships

I consent to act as director of the company named on page 1

Consent signature   **Date**

This section must be signed by either an agent on behalf of all subscribers or the subscribers (i.e those who signed as members on the memorandum of association).

Signed		**Date**
Signed		**Date**
Signed		**Date**
Signed		**Date**
Signed		**Date**
Signed		**Date**
Signed		**Date**

Notes

1. Show for an individual the full forename(s) NOT INITIALS and surname together with any previous forename(s) or surname(s).

   If the director or secretary is a corporation or Scottish firm - show the corporate or firm name on the surname line.

   Give previous forename(s) or surname(s) except that:

   - for a married woman, the name by which she was known before marriage need not be given,

   - names not used since the age of 18 or for at least 20 years need not be given.

   A peer, or an individual known by a title, may state the title instead of or in addition to the forename(s) and surname and need not give the name by which that person was known before he or she adopted the title or succeeded to it.

   Address:

   Give the usual residential address.

   In the case of a corporation or Scottish firm give the registered or principal office.

   Subscribers:

   The form must be signed personally either by the subscriber(s) or by a person or persons authorised to sign on behalf of the subscriber(s).

2. Directors known by another description:

   - A director includes any person who occupies that position even if called by a different name, for example, governor, member of council.

3. Directors details:

   - Show for each individual director the director's date of birth, business occupation and nationality.
   The date of birth must be given for every individual director.

4. Other directorships:

   - Give the name of every company of which the person concerned is a director or has been a director at any time in the past 5 years. You may exclude a company which either **is** or at **all times during the past 5 years,** when the person was a director, **was:**

   - dormant,

   - a parent company which wholly owned the company making the return,

   - a wholly owned subsidiary of the company making the return, or

   - another wholly owned subsidiary of the same parent company.

   If there is insufficient space on the form for other directorships you may use a separate sheet of paper, which should include the company's number and the full name of the director.

5. Use Form 10 continuation sheets or photocopies of page 2 to provide details of joint secretaries or additional directors.

Companies House
— *for the record* —

Please complete in typescript, or in bold black capitals.

CHWP000

12

Declaration on application for registration

Company Name in full

I,

of

† Please delete as appropriate.

do solemnly and sincerely declare that I am a † [Solicitor engaged in the formation of the company][person named as director or secretary of the company in the statement delivered to the Registrar under section 10 of the Companies Act 1985] and that all the requirements of the Companies Act 1985 in respect of the registration of the above company and of matters precedent and incidental to it have been complied with.

And I make this solemn Declaration conscientiously believing the same to be true and by virtue of the Statutory Declarations Act 1835.

Declarant's signature

Declared at

Day	Month	Year

On

❶ Please print name.

before me ❶

Signed **Date**

† A Commissioner for Oaths or Notary Public or Justice of the Peace or Solicitor

You do not have to give any contact information in the box opposite but if you do, it will help Companies House to contact you if there is a query on the form. The contact information that you give will be visible to searchers of the public record.

Tel

DX number   DX exchange

Companies House receipt date barcode

This form has been provided free of charge by Companies House.

Form revised 10/03

When you have completed and signed the form please send it to the Registrar of Companies at:
Companies House, Crown Way, Cardiff, CF14 3UZ   DX 33050 Cardiff
for companies registered in England and Wales
or
Companies House, 37 Castle Terrace, Edinburgh, EH1 2EB
for companies registered in Scotland   DX 235 Edinburgh
                                                   or LP - 4 Edinburgh 2

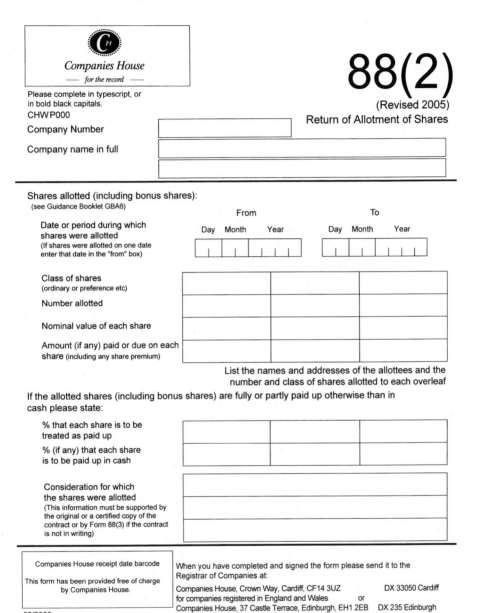

Companies House
— for the record —

Please complete in typescript, or
in bold black capitals.
CHWP000

88(2)
(Revised 2005)
Return of Allotment of Shares

Company Number

Company name in full

Shares allotted (including bonus shares):
(see Guidance Booklet GBA6)

	From			To		
Date or period during which shares were allotted (If shares were allotted on one date enter that date in the "from" box)	Day	Month	Year	Day	Month	Year

Class of shares (ordinary or preference etc)			
Number allotted			
Nominal value of each share			
Amount (if any) paid or due on each share (including any share premium)			

List the names and addresses of the allottees and the
number and class of shares allotted to each overleaf

If the allotted shares (including bonus shares) are fully or partly paid up otherwise than in
cash please state:

% that each share is to be treated as paid up			
% (if any) that each share is to be paid up in cash			

Consideration for which the shares were allotted (This information must be supported by the original or a certified copy of the contract or by Form 88(3) if the contract is not in writing)	

Companies House receipt date barcode

This form has been provided free of charge
by Companies House.

09/2005

When you have completed and signed the form please send it to the
Registrar of Companies at:
Companies House, Crown Way, Cardiff, CF14 3UZ   DX 33050 Cardiff
for companies registered in England and Wales   or
Companies House, 37 Castle Terrace, Edinburgh, EH1 2EB   DX 235 Edinburgh
for companies registered in Scotland   or LP - 4 Edinburgh 2

Names and addresses of the allottees

Shareholder details *(list joint allottees as one shareholder)*	Shares and share class allotted	
	Class of shares allotted	Number allotted
Name(s) _____ Address _____ _____ UK Postcode └ └ └ └ └ └ └	_____ _____ _____	_____ _____ _____
Name(s) _____ Address _____ _____ UK Postcode └ └ └ └ └ └ └	Class of shares allotted _____ _____ _____	Number allotted _____ _____ _____
Name(s) _____ Address _____ _____ UK Postcode └ └ └ └ └ └ └	Class of shares allotted _____ _____ _____	Number allotted _____ _____ _____
Name(s) _____ Address _____ _____ UK Postcode └ └ └ └ └ └ └	Class of shares allotted _____ _____ _____	Number allotted _____ _____ _____
Name(s) _____ Address _____ _____ UK Postcode └ └ └ └ └ └ └	Class of shares allotted _____ _____ _____	Number allotted _____ _____ _____

Please enter the number of continuation sheets (if any) attached to this form

Signed _____ Date _____

** A director / secretary / administrator / administrative receiver / receiver /
official receiver / receiver manager / voluntary arrangement supervisor

*** Please delete as appropriate*

Contact Details

You do not have to give any contact
information in the box opposite but if
you do, it will help Companies House to
contact you if there is a query on the
form. The contact information that you
give will be visible to searchers of the
public record.

	Tel
DX number	DX exchange

Companies House
—— *for the record* ——

Please complete in typescript, or
in bold black capitals.
CHWP000

88(3)

(Revised 2005)

Particulars of a contract relating to shares allotted
as fully or partly paid up otherwise than in cash

Note: This form is only for use where the
contract has not been reduced to writing

Company Number

Company name in full

gives the following particulars of a contract which has not been
reduced to writing

1	Class of Shares (ordinary or preference etc)			
2	The number of shares allotted as fully or partly paid up otherwise than in cash			
3	The nominal value of each such share			
4a	The amount of such nominal value to be considered as paid up on each share otherwise than in cash			
b	The value of each share allotted ie. the nominal value and any premium			
c	The amount to be considered as paid up in respect of b			

continue overleaf

Signed

Date

**Delete as appropriate

** A director / secretary / administrator / administrative receiver / receiver /
official receiver / receiver manager / voluntary arrangement supervisor

Contact Details
You do not have to give any contact
information in the box opposite but if
you do, it will help Companies House to
contact you if there is a query on the
form. The contact information that you
give will be visible to searchers of the
public record.

Tel

DX number   DX exchange

Companies House receipt date barcode

This form has been provided free of charge
by Companies House.

08/2005

When you have completed and signed the form please send it to the
Registrar of Companies at:

Companies House, Crown Way, Cardiff, CF14 3UZ   DX 33050 Cardiff
for companies registered in England and Wales   or
Companies House, 37 Castle Terrace, Edinburgh, EH1 2EB   DX 235 Edinburgh
for companies registered in Scotland   or LP - 4 Edinburgh 2

5 If the consideration for the allotment of such shares is services, or any consideration other than that mentioned in 6,7 or 8 below, state the nature and amount of such consideration, and the number of shares allotted

6 If the allotment is a bonus issue, state the amount of reserves capitalised in respect of this issue

7 If the allotment is made in consideration of the release of a debt, e.g., a director's loan account, state the amount released

8 If the allotment is made in connection with the conversion of loan stock, state the amount of stock converted in respect of this issue

Companies House
— for the record —

190

Location of register of debenture holders

*Please complete in typescript,
or in bold black capitals.*
CHWP000

Company Number

Company Name in full

gives notice that †[a register][registers]†[in duplicate form] of holders of
debentures of the company of the classes mentioned below †[is][are]kept at:

NOTE:
**This notice is not
required where the
register is, and has
always been, kept at
the Registered Office**

Address

Post town

County / region   Postcode

Brief description of class of debentures

Signed   **Date**

† Please delete as appropriate.   † a director / secretary

You do not have to give any contact
information in the box opposite but
if you do, it will help Companies
House to contact you if there is a
query on the form. The contact
information that you give will be
visible to searchers of the public
record.

Tel

DX number   DX exchange

Companies House receipt date barcode

*This form has been provided free of charge
by Companies House.*

Form revised 10/03

When you have completed and signed the form please send it to the
Registrar of Companies at:
Companies House, Crown Way, Cardiff, CF14 3UZ   DX 33050 Cardiff
for companies registered in England and Wales
or
Companies House, 37 Castle Terrace, Edinburgh, EH1 2EB
for companies registered in Scotland   DX 235 Edinburgh
                                                    or LP - 4 Edinburgh 2

G

CHFP000

COMPANIES FORM No. 190a

Notice of place for inspection of a register of holders of debentures which is kept in a non-legible form, or of any change in that place

190a

Please do not write in this margin

Pursuant to the Companies (Registers and Other Records) Regulations 1985

Note: For use only when the register is kept by computer or in some other non-legible form

Please complete legibly, preferably in black type, or bold block lettering

To the Registrar of Companies **(Address overleaf)**

Name of company

For official use

Company number

* insert full name of company

*

gives notice, in accordance with regulation 5(1) of the Companies (Registers and Other Records) Regulations 1985, that the place for inspection of the register of debenture holders which the company keeps in a non-legible form is [now]:

	Postcode

† delete as appropriate

Signed

[Director][Secretary]† Date

Presentor's name address and reference (if any) :

For official Use
General Section

Post room

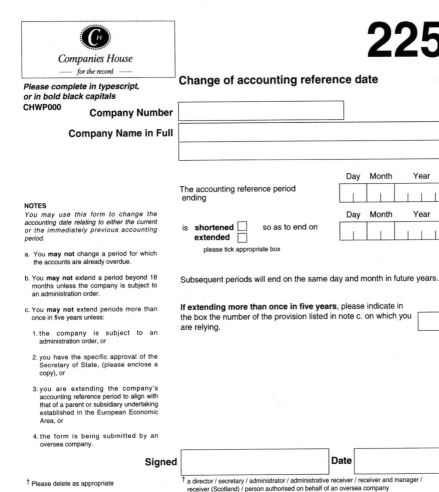

225

Companies House
— for the record —

*Please complete in typescript,
or in bold black capitals*

CHWP000

Change of accounting reference date

Company Number

Company Name in Full

NOTES
*You may use this form to change the
accounting date relating to either the current
or the immediately previous accounting
period.*

a. You **may not** change a period for which
the accounts are already overdue.

b. You **may not** extend a period beyond 18
months unless the company is subject to
an administration order.

c. You **may not** extend periods more than
once in five years unless:

1. the company is subject to an
administration order, or

2. you have the specific approval of the
Secretary of State, (please enclose a
copy), or

3. you are extending the company's
accounting reference period to align with
that of a parent or subsidiary undertaking
established in the European Economic
Area, or

4. the form is being submitted by an
oversea company.

The accounting reference period
ending

Day Month Year

is **shortened** ☐ so as to end on
extended ☐

Day Month Year

please tick appropriate box

Subsequent periods will end on the same day and month in future years.

If extending more than once in five years, please indicate in
the box the number of the provision listed in note c. on which you
are relying.

Signed   **Date**

† Please delete as appropriate

† a director / secretary / administrator / administrative receiver / receiver and manager /
receiver (Scotland) / person authorised on behalf of an oversea company

You do not have to give any contact
information in the box opposite but if
you do, it will help Companies House
to contact you if there is a query on
the form. The contact information that
you give will be visible to searchers of
the public record.

Tel

DX number   DX exchange

Companies House receipt date barcode

*This form has been provided free of charge
by Companies House.*

10/03

When you have completed and signed the form please send it to the
Registrar of Companies at:
Companies House, Crown Way, Cardiff, CF14 3UZ   **DX 33050 Cardiff**
for companies registered in England and Wales   **or**
Companies House, 37 Castle Terrace, Edinburgh, EH1 2EB   **DX 235 Edinburgh**
for companies registered in Scotland   **or LP - 4 Edinburgh 2**

Companies House
— for the record —

287

Change in situation or address of Registered Office

Please complete in typescript,
or in bold black capitals.
CHWP000

Company Number

Company Name in full

New situation of registered office

NOTE:

The change in the
situation of the
registered office does
not take effect until the
Registrar has registered
this notice.

For 14 days beginning
with the date that a
change of registered
office is registered, a
person may validly serve
any document on the
company at its previous
registered office.

PO Box numbers only
are not acceptable.

Address

Post town

County / Region   Postcode

Signed   **Date**

† Please delete as appropriate.

† a director / secretary / administrator / administrative receiver / liquidator / receiver manager / receiver

You do not have to give any contact
information in the box opposite but if
you do, it will help Companies House
to contact you if there is a query on
the form. The contact information
that you give will be visible to
searchers of the public record.

Tel

DX number   DX exchange

Companies House receipt date barcode

This form has been provided free of charge
by Companies House.

10/03

When you have completed and signed the form please send it to the
Registrar of Companies at:
Companies House, Crown Way, Cardiff, CF14 3UZ
for companies registered in England and Wales   or   **DX 33050 Cardiff**
Companies House, 37 Castle Terrace, Edinburgh, EH1 2EB   DX 235 Edinburgh
for companies registered in Scotland   **or LP - 4 Edinburgh 2**

Companies House
—— *for the record* ——

*Please complete in typescript,
or in bold black capitals.*

CHWP000

288a

APPOINTMENT of director or secretary

*(NOT for resignation (use Form 288b) or change
of particulars (use Form 288c))*

Company Number [   ]

Company Name in full [   ]
[   ]

	Day	Month	Year		Day	Month	Year

Date of appointment [| | | | |]   †Date of Birth [| | | | |]

**Appointment
form**

Appointment as director [   ]   as secretary [   ]   Please mark the appropriate box. If appointment is as a director and secretary mark both boxes.

*Notes on completion
appear on reverse.*

NAME   *Style / Title [   ]   *Honours etc [   ]

Forename(s) [   ]

Surname [   ]

Previous Forename(s) [   ]   Previous Surname(s) [   ]

†† Tick this box if the address shown is a service address for the beneficiary of a Confidentiality Order granted under the provisions of section 723B of the Companies Act 1985

†† **Usual residential address** [   ]

[   ]   Post town [   ]   Postcode [   ]

County / Region [   ]   Country [   ]

†Nationality [   ]   †Business occupation [   ]

†Other directorships (additional space overleaf) [   ]

I consent to act as ** director / secretary of the above named company

Consent signature [   ]   **Date** [   ]

* Voluntary details.
† Directors only.
**Delete as appropriate

A director, secretary etc must sign the form below.

Signed [   ]   **Date** [   ]

(**a director / secretary / administrator / administrative receiver / receiver manager / receiver)

You do not have to give any contact information in the box opposite but if you do, it will help Companies House to contact you if there is a query on the form. The contact information that you give will be visible to searchers of the public record.

[   ]

Tel

DX number [   ]   DX exchange [   ]

Companies House receipt date barcode

This form has been provided free of charge by Companies House

Form 10/03

When you have completed and signed the form please send it to the Registrar of Companies at:

Companies House, Crown Way, Cardiff, CF14 3UZ   DX 33050 Cardiff
for companies registered in England and Wales   or
Companies House, 37 Castle Terrace, Edinburgh, EH1 2EB
for companies registered in Scotland   DX 235 Edinburgh
or LP - 4 Edinburgh 2

Company Number

† Directors only.

†Other directorships

NOTES

Show the full forenames, NOT INITIALS. If the director or secretary is a corporation or Scottish firm, show the name on surname line and registered or principal office on the usual residential line.

Give previous forenames or surname(s) except:
- for a married woman, the name by which she was known before marriage need not be given.
- for names not used since the age of 18 or for at least 20 years

A peer or individual known by a title may state the title instead of or in addition to the forenames and surname and need not give the name by which that person was known before he or she adopted the title or succeeded to it.

Other directorships.

Give the name of every company incorporated in Great Britain of which the person concerned is a director or has been a director at any time in the past five years.

You may exclude a company which either is, or at all times during the past five years when the person concerned was a director, was
- dormant
- a parent company which wholly owned the company making the return, or
- another wholly owned subsidiary of the same parent company.

288b

Companies House
— for the record —

Please complete in typescript,
or in bold black capitals.
CHFP000

Terminating appointment as director or secretary
(NOT for appointment (use Form 288a) or change
of particulars (use Form 288c))

Company Number [ ]

Company Name in full [ ]

Date of termination of appointment [Day | Month | Year]

as director [ ] as secretary [ ] *Please mark the appropriate box. If terminating appointment as a director and secretary mark both boxes.*

NAME *Style / Title [ ] *Honours etc [ ]

Please insert details as previously notified to Companies House.

Forename(s) [ ]

Surname [ ]

†Date of Birth [Day | Month | Year]

A serving director, secretary etc must sign the form below.

Signed [ ] **Date** [ ]

* Voluntary details.
† Directors only.
** Delete as appropriate

(** serving director / secretary / administrator / administrative receiver / receiver manager / receiver)

You do not have to give any contact information in the box opposite but if you do, it will help Companies House to contact you if there is a query on the form. The contact information that you give will be visible to searchers of the public record.

Tel [ ]

DX number [ ] DX exchange [ ]

Companies House receipt date barcode

This form has been provided free of charge by Companies House.

10/03

When you have completed and signed the form please send it to the Registrar of Companies at:

Companies House, Crown Way, Cardiff, CF14 3UZ   **DX 33050 Cardiff**
for companies registered in England and Wales   **or**

Companies House, 37 Castle Terrace, Edinburgh, EH1 2EB   **DX 235 Edinburgh**
for companies registered in Scotland   **or LP - 4 Edinburgh 2**

Companies House
—— *for the record* ——

Please complete in typescript,
or in bold black capitals.

CHWP000

288c

CHANGE OF PARTICULARS for director or secretary *(NOT for appointment (use Form 288a) or resignation (use Form 288b))*

Company Number [   ]

Company Name in full [   ]

Changes of particulars form

Complete in all cases

Date of change of particulars

Day	Month	Year

Name   *Style / Title* [   ]   *Honours etc* [   ]

Forename(s) [   ]

Surname [   ]

† Date of Birth

Day	Month	Year

Change of name *(enter new name)* Forename(s) [   ]

Surname [   ]

Change of usual residential address ††

(enter new address)

†† Tick this box if the address shown is a service address for the beneficiary of a Confidentiality Order granted under the provisions of section 723B of the Companies Act 1985

Post town [   ]

County / Region [   ]   Postcode [   ]

Country [   ]

Other change *(please specify)* [   ]

A serving director, secretary etc must sign the form below.

* Voluntary details.
† Directors only.
**Delete as appropriate.

Signed [   ]   **Date** [   ]

(** director / secretary / administrator / administrative receiver / receiver manager / receiver)

You do not have to give any contact information in the box opposite but if you do, it will help Companies House to contact you if there is a query on the form. The contact information that you give will be visible to searchers of the public record..

Tel

DX number   DX exchange

Companies House receipt date barcode

This form has been provided free of charge by Companies House

Form 10/03

When you have completed and signed the form please send it to the Registrar of Companies at:
Companies House, Crown Way, Cardiff, CF14 3UZ   DX 33050 Cardiff
for companies registered in England and Wales   or
Companies House, 37 Castle Terrace, Edinburgh, EH1 2EB
for companies registered in Scotland   DX 235 Edinburgh
or LP - 4 Edinburgh 2

Companies House
— *for the record* —

318

Location of directors' service contracts

Please complete in typescript,
or in bold black capitals.

CHFP000

Company Number

Company Name in full

Address where directors' service contracts
or memoranda are available for inspection
by members.

NOTE:
Directors' service
contracts **MUST** be kept
at an address in the
country of incorporation.

This notice is not
required where the
relevant documents are
and have always been
kept at the Registered
Office.

Address

Post town

County / Region   **Postcode**

Signed   **Date**

† Please delete as appropriate.

† a director / secretary / administrator / administrative receiver / receiver manager / receiver

Please give the name, address,
telephone number and, if available,
a DX number and Exchange of
the person Companies House should
contact if there is any query.

Tel

DX number   DX exchange

Companies House receipt date barcode

This form has been provided free of charge
by Companies House.

Form revised July 1998

When you have completed and signed the form please send it to the
Registrar of Companies at:
Companies House, Crown Way, Cardiff, CF14 3UZ   DX 33050 Cardiff
for companies registered in England and Wales
or
Companies House, 37 Castle Terrace, Edinburgh, EH1 2EB
for companies registered in Scotland   **DX 235 Edinburgh**

Companies House
—— *for the record* ——

325

Location of register of directors' interests in shares etc.

Please complete in typescript,
or in bold black capitals.

CHFP000

Company Number

Company Name in full

The register of directors' interests in shares and/or debentures is kept at:

NOTE:
The register **MUST** be kept at an address in the country of incorporation.

This notice is not required where the register is and has always been kept at the Registered Office.

Address

Post town

County / Region   **Postcode**

Signed   **Date**

† Please delete as appropriate.

† a director / secretary / administrator / administrative receiver / receiver manager / receiver

Please give the name, address, telephone number and, if available, a DX number and Exchange of the person Companies House should contact if there is any query.

Tel

DX number   DX exchange

Companies House receipt date barcode

This form has been provided free of charge by Companies House.

When you have completed and signed the form please send it to the Registrar of Companies at:
Companies House, Crown Way, Cardiff, CF14 3UZ   **DX 33050 Cardiff**
for companies registered in England and Wales
or
Companies House, 37 Castle Terrace, Edinburgh, EH1 2EB
for companies registered in Scotland   **DX 235 Edinburgh**

Form revised July 1998

G

CHFP000

COMPANIES FORM No. 325a

Notice of place for inspection of a register of directors' interests in shares etc. which is kept in a non-legible form, or of any change in that place

325a

Pursuant to the Companies (Registers and Other Records) Regulations 1985

Note: For use only when the register is kept by computer or in some other non-legible form

To the Registrar of Companies
(Address overleaf)

For official use   Company number

Name of company

*

gives notice, in accordance with regulation 3(1) of the Companies (Registers and Other Records)
Regulations 1985, that the place for inspection of the register of directors' interests in shares and/or

debentures which the company keeps in a non-legible form is [now] †:

Postcode

Signed   [Director][Secretary]† Date

Presentor's name address and reference (if any) :

For official Use
General Section   Post room

Companies House
—— *for the record* ——

Register of members

353

*Please complete in typescript,
or in bold black capitals.*

CHWP000

Company Number

Company Name in full

The register of members is kept at:

NOTE:
The register **MUST** be kept at an address in the country of incorporation.

This notice is not required where the register has, at all times since it came into existence (or in the case of a register in existence on 1 July 1948 at all times since then) been kept at the registered office.

Address

Post town

County / Region   **Postcode**

Signed   **Date**

† Please delete as appropriate.

† a director / secretary / administrator / administrative receiver / receiver manager / receiver

You do not have to give any contact information in the box opposite but if you do, it will help Companies House to contact you if there is a query on the form. The contact information that you give will be visible to searchers of the public record.

Tel

DX number   DX exchange

Companies House receipt date barcode

This form has been provided free of charge by Companies House.

Form revised 10/03

When you have completed and signed the form please send it to the Registrar of Companies at:
Companies House, Crown Way, Cardiff, CF14 3UZ   DX 33050 Cardiff
for companies registered in England and Wales
or
Companies House, 37 Castle Terrace, Edinburgh, EH1 2EB
for companies registered in Scotland   DX 235 Edinburgh
or LP - 4 Edinburgh 2

G

CHFP000

COMPANIES FORM No. 353a

Notice of place for inspection of a register of members which is kept in a non-legible form, or of any change in that place

353a

Please do not write in this margin

Pursuant to the Companies (Registers and Other Records) Regulations 1985

Note: For use only when the register is kept by computer or in some other non-legible form

Please complete legibly, preferably in black type, or bold block lettering

To the Registrar of Companies **(Address overleaf)**

For official use

Company number

Name of company

* insert full name of company

*

gives notice, in accordance with regulation 3(1) of the Companies (Registers and Other Records)

Regulations 1985, that the place for inspection of the register of members of the company which the

† delete as appropriate

company keeps in a non-legible form is [now] †:

Postcode

Signed   [Director][Secretary]†   Date

Presentor's name address and reference (if any) :

For official Use
General Section

Post room

Companies House
— *for the record* —

*Please complete in typescript,
or in bold black capitals.*

CHFP000

363a

Annual Return

Company Number |

Company Name in full |

|

Date of this return

The information in this return is made up to

| Day | Month | Year |

|__ __|/|__ __|/|__ __ __ __|

Date of next return

If you wish to make your next return
to a date earlier than the anniversary
of this return please show the date here.
Companies House will then send a form
at the appropriate time.

| Day | Month | Year |

|__ __|/|__ __|/|__ __ __ __|

Registered Office

Show here the address **at the date of
this return.**

*Any change of
registered office*
must *be notified
on form 287.*

|

|

Post town |

County / Region |

UK Postcode |__ __ __ __| |__ __ __|

Principal business activities

Show trade classification code number(s)
for the principal activity or activities.

|_____| |_____|

|_____| |_____|

If the code number cannot be determined,
give a brief description of principal activity.

|

|

Companies House receipt date barcode

*This form has been provided free of charge
by Companies House*

Form April 2002

When you have completed and signed the form please send it to the
Registrar of Companies at:

Companies House, Crown Way, Cardiff, CF14 3UZ   DX 33050 Cardiff
for companies registered in England and Wales
or
Companies House, 37 Castle Terrace, Edinburgh, EH1 2EB
for companies registered in Scotland   **DX 235 Edinburgh**

Page 1

Register of members

If the register of members is not kept at the registered office, state here where it is kept.

Post town

County / Region _____ UK Postcode └ └ └ └ └ └ └

Register of Debenture holders

If there is a register of debenture holders, or a duplicate of any such register or part of it, which is not kept at the registered office, state here where it is kept.

Post town

County / Region _____ UK Postcode └ └ └ └ └ └ └

Company type

Public limited company	☐
Private company limited by shares	☐
Private company limited by guarantee without share capital	☐
Private company limited by shares exempt under section 30	☐
Private company limited by guarantee exempt under section 30	☐
Private unlimited company with share capital	☐
Private unlimited company without share capital	☐

> Please tick the appropriate box

Company Secretary

* Voluntary details.

(Please photocopy this area to provide details of joint secretaries).

†† **Tick this box if the address shown is a service address for the beneficiary of a Confidentiality Order granted under section 723B of the Companies Act 1985 otherwise, give your usual residential address. In the case of a corporation or Scottish firm, give the registered or principal office address.**

If a partnership give the names and addresses of the partners or the name of the partnership and office address.

Details of a new company secretary must be notified on form 288a.

Name   * Style / Title

Forename(s)

Surname

Address ††

Post town

County / Region   UK Postcode └ └ └ └ └ └ └

Country

Directors

Please list directors in alphabetical order.

Details of new directors must be notified on form 288a

Name	*** Style / Title**

Directors In the case of a director that is a corporation or a Scottish firm, the name is the corporate or firm name.

†† Tick this box if the address shown is a service address for the beneficiary of a Confidentiality Order granted under section 723B of the Companies Act 1985 otherwise, give your usual residential address. In the case of a corporation or Scottish firm, give the registered or principal office address.

Day   Month   Year

Date of birth ∟∟/∟∟/∟∟∟∟

Forename(s)

Surname

Address ††

Post town

County / Region   UK Postcode ∟∟∟∟   ∟∟∟

Country   **Nationality**

Business occupation

* Voluntary details.

Name	*** Style / Title**

Directors In the case of a director that is a corporation or a Scottish firm, the name is the corporate or firm name.

†† Tick this box if the address shown is a service address for the beneficiary of a Confidentiality Order granted under section 723B of the Companies Act 1985 otherwise, give your usual residential address. In the case of a corporation or Scottish firm, give the registered or principal office address.

Day   Month   Year

Date of birth ∟∟/∟∟/∟∟∟∟

Forename(s)

Surname

Address ††

Post town

County / Region   UK Postcode ∟∟∟∟   ∟∟∟

Country   **Nationality**

Business occupation

Class *(e.g. Ordinary/Preference)*	Number of shares issued	Aggregate Nominal Value *(i.e Number of shares issued multiplied by nominal value per share, or total amount of stock)*

Issued share capital
Enter details of all the shares in issue
at the date of this return.

|_____	|_____	|_____
|_____	|_____	|_____
|_____	|_____	|_____
|_____	|_____	|_____
Totals	|_____	|_____

List of past and present shareholders
(Use attached schedule where appropriate)
A full list is required if one was not
included with either of the last two
returns.

There were no changes in the period ☐

	on paper	in another format
A list of changes is enclosed	☐	☐
A full list of shareholders is enclosed	☐	☐

Certificate

I certify that the information given in this return is true to the best of my
knowledge and belief.

Signed [_____]   **Date** [_____]

† Please delete as appropriate.   † a director /secretary

When you have signed the return send it
with the fee to the Registrar of
Companies. Cheques should be made
payable to **Companies House.**

This return includes [_____] continuation sheets.
(enter number)

You do not have to give any contact
information in the box opposite but if
you do, it will help Companies House to
contact you if there is a query on the
form. The contact information that you
give will be visible to searchers of the
public record.

|_____

|_____

|_____ Tel |_____

DX number |_____ DX exchange |_____

Directors

Details of new directors must be notified on form 288a

Please list directors in alphabetical order.

Name * Style / Title

Directors In the case of a director that is a corporation or a Scottish firm, the name is the corporate or firm name.

Day   Month   Year

Date of birth |__|__|/|__|__|/|__|__|__|__|

Forename(s)

†† Tick this box if the address shown is a service address for the beneficiary of a Confidentiality Order granted under section 723B of the Companies Act 1985 otherwise, give your usual residential address. In the case of a corporation or Scottish firm, give the registered or principal office address.

Surname

Address ††

Post town

County / Region   UK Postcode |__|__|__|__| |__|__|__|

Country   **Nationality**

Business occupation

* Voluntary details.

Name * Style / Title

Directors In the case of a director that is a corporation or a Scottish firm, the name is the corporate or firm name.

Day   Month   Year

Date of birth |__|__|/|__|__|/|__|__|__|__|

Forename(s)

†† Tick this box if the address shown is a service address for the beneficiary of a Confidentiality Order granted under section 723B of the Companies Act 1985 otherwise, give your usual residential address. In the case of a corporation or Scottish firm, give the registered or principal office address.

Surname

Address ††

Post town

County / Region   UK Postcode |__|__|__|__| |__|__|__|

Country   **Nationality**

Business occupation

Directors

Please list directors in alphabetical order.

Details of new directors must be notified on form 288a

Name * Style / Title

Directors In the case of a director that is a corporation or a Scottish firm, the name is the corporate or firm name.

†† **Tick this box if the address shown is a service address for the beneficiary of a Confidentiality Order granted under section 723B of the Companies Act 1985 otherwise, give your usual residential address. In the case of a corporation or Scottish firm, give the registered or principal office address.**

Day Month Year

Date of birth

Forename(s)

Surname

Address ††

Post town

County / Region UK Postcode

Country **Nationality**

Business occupation

* Voluntary details.

Name * Style / Title

Directors In the case of a director that is a corporation or a Scottish firm, the name is the corporate or firm name.

†† **Tick this box if the address shown is a service address for the beneficiary of a Confidentiality Order granted under section 723B of the Companies Act 1985 otherwise, give your usual residential address. In the case of a corporation or Scottish firm, give the registered or principal office address.**

Day Month Year

Date of birth

Forename(s)

Surname

Address ††

Post town

County / Region UK Postcode

Country **Nationality**

Business occupation

List of past and present shareholders (Continued)

Company Number |_____

Shareholders' details	Class and number of shares or amount of stock held	Shares or amount of stock transferred *(if appropriate)*	
		Class and number of shares or amount of stock transferred	Date of registration of transfer
Name |.. Address |.. |.. |.. UK Postcode ⌐ ⌐ ⌐ ⌐ ⌐ ⌐ ⌐			
Name |.. Address |.. |.. |.. UK Postcode ⌐ ⌐ ⌐ ⌐ ⌐ ⌐ ⌐			
Name |.. Address |.. |.. |.. UK Postcode ⌐ ⌐ ⌐ ⌐ ⌐ ⌐ ⌐			
Name |.. Address |.. |.. |.. UK Postcode ⌐ ⌐ ⌐ ⌐ ⌐ ⌐ ⌐			
Name |.. Address |.. |.. |.. UK Postcode ⌐ ⌐ ⌐ ⌐ ⌐ ⌐ ⌐			

Companies House
—— *for the record* ——

Please complete in typescript,
or in bold black capitals.
CHFP000

391

Notice of passing of resolution removing an auditor

Company Number [   ]

Company Name in full [   ]
[   ]

Date of resolution

Day	Month		Year	

Date of removal

Day	Month		Year	

Details of auditor removed from office [   ]

Firm / Partnership / Individual [   ]

Address [   ]
[   ]

Post town [   ]

County / Region [   ]   Postcode [   ]

Signed [   ]   **Date** [   ]

† Please delete as appropriate.   † a director / secretary

Please give the name, address,
telephone number and, if available,
a DX number and Exchange of
the person Companies House should
contact if there is any query.

[   ]
[   ]
| Tel |
| DX number | DX exchange |

Companies House receipt date barcode

This form has been provided free of charge
by Companies House.

Form revisedJuly 1998

When you have completed and signed the form please send it to the
Registrar of Companies at:
Companies House, Crown Way, Cardiff, CF14 3UZ   DX 33050 Cardiff
for companies registered in England and Wales
or
Companies House, 37 Castle Terrace, Edinburgh, EH1 2EB
for companies registered in Scotland   **DX 235 Edinburgh**

COMPANIES FORM No. 403a

**Declaration of satisfaction
in full or in part
of mortgage or charge**

CHWP000

403a

Please do not
write in
this margin

Pursuant to section 403(1) of the Companies Act 1985

*Please complete
legibly, preferably
in black type, or
bold block lettering*

To the Registrar of Companies
(Address overleaf)

For official use   Company number

Name of company

* insert full name
of company

*

I, _____

of _____

† delete as
appropriate

[a director][the secretary][the administrator][the administrative receiver]† of the above company, do
solemnly and sincerely declare that the debt for which the charge described below was given has been
paid or satisfied in **[full][part]†**

insert a description
of the instrument(s)
creating or
evidencing the
charge, eg
"Mortgage",
'Charge',
'Debenture' etc

Date and description of charge # _____

Date of registration ø _____

Name and address of [chargee][trustee for the debenture holders]† _____

ø the date of
registration may be
confirmed from the
certificate

Short particulars of property charged § _____

§ insert brief details
of property

And I make this solemn declaration conscientiously believing the same to be true and by virtue of the
provisions of the Statutory Declarations Act 1835.

Declared at _____   Declarant to sign below

| Day | Month | Year |
on

before me _____
A Commissioner for Oaths or Notary Public or Justice of
the Peace or a Solicitor having the powers conferred on a
Commissioner for Oaths.

Presentor's name address and
reference (if any) :

For official Use (10/03)
Mortgage Section

Post room

M

CHFP000

Please do not
write in
this margin

COMPANIES FORM No. 403b

**Declaration that part of the
property or undertaking charged
(a) has been released from the
charge; (b) no longer forms part of
the company's property or undertaking**

403b

Pursuant to section 403(1) (b) of the Companies Act 1985

*Please complete
legibly, preferably
in black type, or
bold block lettering*

* insert full name
of company

To the Registrar of Companies
(Address overleaf)

Name of company

For official use   Company number

*

I, _____

of _____

† delete as
appropriate

insert a description
of the instrument(s)
creating or
evidencing the
charge, eg
"Mortgage',
'Charge',
'Debenture' etc

ø the date of
registration may be
confirmed from the
certificate

§ insert brief details
of property or
undertaking no
longer subject to
the charge

[a director][the secretary][the administrator][the administrative receiver]† of the above company, do
solemnly and sincerely declare that with respect to the charge described below the part of the property
or undertaking described [has been released from the charge][has ceased to form part of the
company's property or undertaking]†

Date and description of charge # _____

Date of registration ø _____

Name and address of [chargee][trustee for the debenture holders]† _____

_____

Short particulars of property or undertaking released or no longer part of the company's property or
undertaking § _____

_____

And I make this solemn declaration conscientiously believing the same to be true and by virtue of the
provisions of the Statutory Declarations Act 1835.

Declared at _____

_____

Declarant to sign below

on

Day	Month	Year

before me _____

A Commissioner for Oaths or Notary Public or Justice of
the Peace or a Solicitor having the powers conferred on a
Commissioner for Oaths.

Presentor's name address and
reference (if any) :

For official Use (02/00)
Mortgage Section

Post room

Companies House
— *for the record* —

*Please complete in typescript,
or in bold black capitals*

CHWP000

652a

Application for striking off

Company Number	
Company Name In Full	

I/We as **DIRECTOR(S)** apply for this company to be struck off the register.

In the past three months the company has not:

- traded or otherwise carried on business, or changed its name;
- disposed of for value any property or rights which it would have disposed of for value in the normal course of trading or carrying on business; or
- engaged in any other activity except for the purpose of making this application, settling its affairs or meeting a statutory requirement.

This company is not the subject of, nor the proposed subject of, insolvency proceedings or a section 425 scheme.

I/We enclose the fee of £10 (made payable to Companies House).

Director signatures (use continuation sheet if necessary).

WARNING: TO ALL APPLICANTS

IT IS AN OFFENCE KNOWINGLY OR RECKLESSLY TO PROVIDE FALSE OR MISLEADING INFORMATION ON THIS APPLICATION. YOU ARE ADVISED TO READ THE NOTES OVERLEAF AND TO CONSULT THE GUIDANCE NOTES AVAILABLE FROM COMPANIES HOUSE BEFORE COMPLETING THIS FORM. IF IN DOUBT, SEEK PROFESSIONAL ADVICE.

WARNING: TO ALL INTERESTED PARTIES.

THIS IS AN IMPORTANT NOTICE AND SHOULD NOT BE IGNORED. THE COMPANY NAMED HAS APPLIED TO THE REGISTRAR TO BE STRUCK OFF THE REGISTER AND DISSOLVED. ON DISSOLUTION ANY REMAINING ASSETS WILL PASS TO THE CROWN. THE REGISTRAR WILL STRIKE THE COMPANY OFF THE REGISTER UNLESS HE HAS REASONABLE CAUSE NOT TO DO SO. GUIDANCE NOTES ARE AVAILABLE ON GROUNDS FOR OBJECTION. IF IN DOUBT, SEEK PROFESSIONAL ADVICE.

Name of Director		
Signed		Date
Name of Director		
Signed		Date
Name of Director		
Signed		Date

You do not have to give any contact information in the box opposite but if you do, it will help Companies House to contact you if there is a query on the form. The contact information that you give will be visible to searchers of the public

Tel
DX number   DX exchange

Companies House receipt date barcode

This form has been provided free of charge by Companies House.

Form revised 10/03

When you have signed the form send it with the fee to the Registrar of Companies at:

Companies House, Crown Way, Cardiff, CF14 3UZ   DX 33050 Cardiff
for companies registered in England and Wales
or
Companies House, 37 Castle Terrace Edinburgh, EH1 2EB
for companies registered in Scotland   DX 235 Edinburgh
                                          or LP - 4 Edinburgh 2

Notes:

Guidance notes on all aspects of striking off are available from Companies House. You are advised to read them fully BEFORE completing and returning this form.

If the company ceases to be eligible for striking off at any time after the application is made, then the application must be withdrawn using form 652c. Failure to do so is an offence.

Copies of this application must be sent to all notifiable parties i.e. creditors, employees, shareholders, pension managers or trustees and other directors of the company within 7 days from the day on which the application is made. Copies must also be sent to anyone who later becomes a notifiable party within 7 days of becoming so. You should check the guidance notes which contain a full list of those who must be notified. Failure to notify interested parties is an offence. It is advisable to obtain and retain some proof of delivery or posting of copies to notifiable parties.

This form must be signed by the sole director, by both if there are two, or by the majority if there are more than two. If more than three directors' signatures are required, continuation sheets for this form are available from Companies House.

Companies House
—— *for the record* ——

652a cont

Please complete in typescript, or in bold black capitals
CHWP000

Application for striking off (continuation sheet)

Company Number

Company Name In Full

WARNING: TO ALL APPLICANTS

IT IS AN OFFENCE KNOWINGLY OR RECKLESSLY TO PROVIDE FALSE OR MISLEADING INFORMATION ON THIS APPLICATION. YOU ARE ADVISED TO READ THE NOTES OVERLEAF AND TO CONSULT THE GUIDANCE NOTES AVAILABLE FROM COMPANIES HOUSE BEFORE COMPLETING THIS FORM. IF IN DOUBT, SEEK PROFESSIONAL ADVICE.

WARNING: TO ALL INTERESTED PARTIES.

THIS IS AN IMPORTANT NOTICE AND SHOULD NOT BE IGNORED. THE COMPANY NAMED HAS APPLIED TO THE REGISTRAR TO BE STRUCK OFF THE REGISTER AND DISSOLVED. ON DISSOLUTION ANY REMAINING ASSETS WILL PASS TO THE CROWN. THE REGISTRAR WILL STRIKE THE COMPANY OFF THE REGISTER UNLESS HE HAS REASONABLE CAUSE NOT TO DO SO. GUIDANCE NOTES ARE AVAILABLE ON GROUNDS FOR OBJECTION. IF IN DOUBT, SEEK PROFESSIONAL ADVICE.

NAME

SIGNATURE   DATE

NAME

SIGNATURE   DATE

NAME

SIGNATURE   DATE

NAME

SIGNATURE   DATE

NAME

SIGNATURE   DATE

NAME

SIGNATURE   DATE

NAME

SIGNATURE   DATE

NAME

SIGNATURE   DATE

NAME

SIGNATURE   DATE

July 1998

Companies House
—— *for the record* ——

652c

Withdrawal of application for striking off

Please complete in typescript,
or in bold black capitals

CHWP000

Company Number

Company Name In Full

The directors hereby withdraw the application dated

in which it was requested that this company be struck off the register.

This form can be
signed by any
director.

Name

Signed

Date

You do not have to give any contact
information in the box opposite but
if you do, it will help Companies
House to contact you if there is a
query on the form. The contact
information that you give will be
visible to searchers of the public
record.

Tel

DX number   DX exchange

Companies House receipt date barcode

This form has been provided free of
charge by Companies House.

Form revised 10/03

When you have signed the form send it to the Registrar of Companies at:
Companies House, Crown Way, Cardiff, CF14 3UZ   DX 33050 Cardiff
for companies registered in England and Wales
or
Companies House, 37 Castle Terrace, Edinburgh, EH1 2EB
for companies registered in Scotland   DX 235 Edinburgh
                                               or LP - 4 Edinburgh 2

Appendix 2:

Useful addresses

Companies House Addresses
English/Welsh Companies
Companies House
Crown Way
Cardiff
CF14 3UZ
Tel: 0870 333 3636
Fax: 029 203 80900

The London Information Centre
21 Bloomsbury Street
London
WC1B 3XD
Tel: 0870 333 3636
Fax: 020 7637 6210

Scottish Companies
Edinburgh Information Centre
37 Castle Terrace
Edinburgh
EH1 2EB
Tel: 0870 333 3636
Fax: 029 203 80900

Worthing Stamp Office (postal
applications only)
Room 35, East Block
Barrington Road
Worthing
BN12 4XJ
Tel: 0845 60 30 135

London Stamp Office (personal
callers only)
South West Wing, Bush House
Strand
London
WC2B 4QN
Tel: 020 7438 7252/7452

Edinburgh Stamp Office (postal and
fax only)
Grayfield House
Spur X, 5 Bankhead Avenue
Edinburgh
EH11 4BF
Fax: 0131 442 3030

Business Link
website: www.businesslink.gov.uk

**Data Protection
    Registration Office**
Wyclisse House
Water Lane
Wilmslow
Cheshire
SK9 5AX
Tel: 01625 545745
website: www.dataprotection.gov.uk

**Institute of Chartered
    Accountants in England
    and Wales**
PO Box 433
Chartered Accountants Hall
Moorgate Place
London
EC2P 2BJ
Tel: 0207 920 8100

**Institute of Chartered Secretaries
    and Administrators**
16 Park Crescent
London
W1B 1AH
Tel: 0207 580 4741

The Law Society
113 Chancery Lane
London
WC2A 1PL
Tel: 0207 242 1222

**Trade Marks, Patents and
    Design Registry**
The Patent Office
Cardiff Road
Newport
Gwent
NP10 8QQ
Tel: 0845 9500 505

**Institute of Trade Mark
    Attorneys**
4th Floor
Canterbury House
2–6 Sydenham Road
Croydon
Surrey
CR0 9XE
Tel: 0208 686 2052

Appendix 3:

Deregulation of private companies

Useful hints to cut red tape

Method	Description	Chapter(s)
Audit exemption	Certain companies are no longer required to have an audit if the company meets certain criteria	7
Elective resolutions	Purpose: – indefinite authority for directors to allot shares – to dispense with circulating accounts prior to a general meeting – to dispense with annual general meetings – to reduce the majority of shareholders required to call an EGM (to 90 per cent)	7, 8
Directors' and officers' insurance to limit liability	Check that the Articles of Association allow for the directors to take out this type of insurance	2

Method	Description	Chapter(s)
Optional company seal	Under the Companies Act the seal is now optional. The provision is as follows: *A document signed by a director and the secretary of a company, or by two directors and expressed (in whatever form of words) to be executed by the company has the same effect as if executed under the common seal of the company.* – if the document executed is a deed, include the words *Executed as a deed* in the text	1, 6
Sole shareholder	Single member companies are now allowed. This is useful for 100 per cent owned subsidiaries. **NB**. Decisions of sole shareholder should still be recorded, signed and dated	2, 6
Trade mark registration	Consider for name protection. Search Trade Mark Registry when investigating new company names. **NB**. Can now register shape, packaging, sounds and smells!	3
Written resolutions of shareholders	This can be useful where it is in-convenient to hold a general meeting. There are two methods: (a) Can be allowed under company's Articles of Association (Table A, clause 53 1985) (b) Allowed under the Companies Act 1985 (cannot be used to remove a director or auditor) **NB**. Some additional provisions are made for certain events.	8

Bibliography

Companies House provide a series of leaflets entitled *Notes for Guidance*, including:

Accounts and Accounting Reference Dates – GBA3

Auditors – GBA4

Late Filing Penalties – GBA5

Resolutions – GBA7

Company Names – GBF2

Liquidation and Insolvency – GBW1

Liquidation and Insolvency (Scotland) – GBW1(S)

Strike-off, Dissolution and Restoration – GBW2

Company legislation

Companies Acts 1985 and 1989

Insolvency Act 1986

Company Directors Disqualification Act 1986

Deregulation and Contracting Out Act 1994

The Combined Code on Corporate Governance issued by the Financial Reporting Council (in force from June 2004)

The Directors' Remuneration Report Regulations 2002

Butterworths Company Law Handbook, 18th edn, 2005, Butterworth Law

Forming a Limited Company, 7th edn, 2001, P Clayton, Kogan Page

Duties of a Company Secretary, Institute of Chartered Secretaries and Administrators

A Short Guide to the Retention of Documents, Andrew C Hamer, ICSA

A list of books for business is available from the publishers at the address below:

Kogan Page Limited
120 Pentonville Road
London
N1 9JN
Tel: 0207 278 0433
Fax: 0207 837 6348

Index

NB: page numbers in italic indicate figures or tables

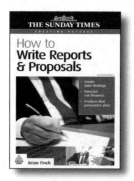

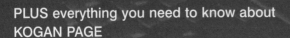